# *Ways to Improve Your Study Habits*

by
**Stephen Edwards**

*Information to Encourage Achievement*

1261 West Glenlake
Chicago, IL 60660
*www.encouragementpress.com*

ISBN: 1-933766-04-2
EAN: 978-1-933766-04-1

10 9 8 7 6 5 4 3 2 1
♻ printed on recycled paper

©2007 Encouragement Press, LLC
1261 West Glenlake
Chicago, IL 60660

# *Ways to Improve Your Study Habits*

# About the Author

For more than 20 years, Stephen Edwards has been a regular contributor on a variety of consumer and business subjects, including books and articles about freelancing, starting a new business and marketing your company. In addition to Encouragement Press, Mr. Edwards has worked with publishers such as Probus Publishing, Times Mirror, McGraw Hill, Dartnell, Thompson International, Socrates Media and Scott Foresman and associations such as the American Medical Association, American Hospital Association and American Association of Neurological Surgeons.

Along with the title of accomplished author, Mr. Edwards is also a successful marketing consultant and graphic artist. A graduate of Indiana University, Mr. Edwards earned his business degrees in Management Administration and Marketing.

# Acknowledgements

Special thanks . . . and cheers to the following:

Heather Hutchins and Steven Pincich

# Table of Contents

# Introduction

Learning to study is like learning to ride a bike—once you get it you have the skills for life. But that does not mean that there are not bumps and bruises along the way. There sure are and it is no easy task to learn (or relearn for older students) how to make yourself into a studying machine.

*50 plus one Ways to Improve Your Study Habits* is written for a variety of students—or anyone who wants to return to school and may be a bit rusty on the study habits front. Junior high and high school students, part-time and full-time college and graduate students, parents and guardians—even teachers and tutors will find a vast storehouse of tips, techniques and solutions to a variety of studying related problems and obstacles.

Imagine being able to overcome procrastination, fear of writing papers, poor vocabulary, test anxiety, conducting research and a host of problems that might prevent you from doing your best. Well, the fact is that these and other barriers to personal success can and will be overcome by using the hundreds of practical and easy-to-implement hints provided. You can be the academic star, even if you have not stepped foot in a school for years!

You can replace bad habits with good ones. You can learn how to motivate and reward yourself. You will learn how to break lengthy and difficult tasks (like writing a research report) into manageable tasks. You will learn how to use your time more effectively. You can learn how to use the Internet to increase your productivity and decrease your work load. You will learn how to use all the resources available to you—study groups, tutors, friends, family and your instructors to turn average grades into excellent grades.

The techniques and strategies presented in this book are the best ones that educators and experts have culled from their years of experience of teaching and coaching students of all ages. The habits learned from this book can be used not only in school, but on the job as well. They will become life habits that will assist in your personal and professional development.

If you learn to study properly, you will gain time, energy and self-confidence. Learn to learn and enjoy the benefits!

Stephen Edwards

# *plus one*

## Setting Up Your Goals

A very popular senior is finding it difficult to become a good student. She used to be more interested in parties than studying, but she now realizes the error of her ways. Unfortunately, she is not having much success. Every week, she vows to spend more time studying, but she finds that her life goes so quickly that she does not think about it until shortly before bedtime. She is having trouble achieving her goal, but she does not know how to change her life, her schedule or her behavior.

### The Challenge

Setting goals is the basic building block of accomplishing any project. Students who learn this skill in school can use their expertise over and over again in their careers. Surprisingly, many managers and high-level employees are no more successful at setting goals.

Anyone can learn to set goals, work toward them and achieve them. All that is required is a little time to think, plan and visualize. In addition, like plants, you have to keep an eye on your goals and nourish them from time to time.

### The Facts

A goal can be defined as something we want to have, to achieve or to accomplish. Goals give a specific focus to our energy and help us to know exactly what to do to make our dreams come true.

Here are three good reasons to learn how to set and manage your goals:

1. Goals help you control your time and energy.
   Goals give people a sense of purpose and a focus. If you have specific goals, you know exactly what you need to do from day to day. In a sense, goals can be a compass for your life.

2. Goals help you get more done.
   Research shows that those people who create and maintain a list of goals get more done in their lives than those without a formal goal-setting

strategy. In addition, as you set goals and achieve them, you will improve your self-confidence.

3. Goals help you motivate yourself.

Goals can be used as road signs to help you figure out the path ahead. They also can be a way of challenging yourself to achieve bigger and better things. Part of the process of setting goals is mapping out how you will accomplish them. Goal setting involves breaking the overall goal into small, manageable chunks.

Your goals should be performance-based rather than outcome-based. An example of an outcome-based goal might be getting an A in all of your math courses. The problem with this goal is that there are many things that are outside of your control. You may study diligently, but you could be sick on the day of an important exam. In addition, the teacher may have created an especially difficult exam or have given out instructions that were confusing.

The corresponding performance-based goal would be that you will improve your math scores by studying every night for 1 hour, working with a math tutor and creating a math study group. Notice that all of these tasks are within your control. You will be the one making them happen.

## The Solutions

Setting goals is not an easy task, but you will get better at it with practice. The following seven goal-setting tips will help you to create goals that you can achieve:

Goal 1: Goals need to be precise and measurable.

You want to be able to figure out easily whether you met your goal or not. Create goals that include exact amounts and due dates. For example, one study goal might be to improve your English paper grades by starting every paper 3 weeks ahead of the due date, working with a tutor in the writing center 2 days a week and having your sister, the English major, proof every paper before you turn it in. Notice that every part of this goal is specific. In addition, your goal needs specific and measurable sub-points that explain the steps you will take to accomplish the goal.

Goal 2: You need both long-term and short-term goals.

Long-term goals can be goals for your whole life, your career or your retirement. They also may include goals for the next year, 6 months or semester. Short-term goals are based on the long-term goals, but they included the day-to-day details. These are usually monthly, weekly and daily goals.

For example, maybe your goal for the semester is to create a study schedule for each class and stick to it at least 75 percent of the time. Your short-term goals would involve creating monthly, weekly and daily study schedules and keeping track of your adherence to the schedule.

Goal 3: Goals need to be flexible.

Goals change just as people do. You need to understand that your goals will change over time, and you need to be able to update them. For example, you may begin the semester with a goal of spending extra study time on your math class. After you earn an A on your midterm examination, you may decide that you already have achieved your goal and that you need to spend that extra study time on your English class. If you achieve your goal before the semester is out, you need to be flexible enough to acknowledge that you have done what you set out to do and then set a new goal.

Goal 4: Goals need to be realistic but challenging.

You need to find a balance between creating goals that you can actually achieve and challenging yourself. If your goal is too easy, it will not motivate you very much. By the same token, if your goal is so challenging that you cannot even come close to achieving it, you run the risk of damaging your self-confidence.

For example, if you had a goal of keeping a semester-long study schedule 75 percent of the time, you might adapt the goal, depending upon how difficult your classes are. If you found that the goal was not challenging enough because you already were keeping to your study schedule 80 percent of the time, you should adjust the goal or create a more challenging one.

On the other hand, if you found that you were keeping to your schedule only 50 percent of the time, you might decide to adjust the percentage downward so that you would have a better chance of being successful. It is difficult to feel motivated if you think that you will never reach your goal.

Goal 5: Goals need to be meaningful to you.

Just as with rewards, goals need to be meaningful to you. You cannot allow anyone else to set your goals because other people's goals will not motivate you. Choose goals that matter to you and that you believe you can accomplish. For example, if you find that you procrastinate about studying for your history tests, you can set a goal of studying history for 1 hour each day for 2 weeks prior to the exam. Although 1 hour a day may not seem like much time, you want to set a goal that you can accomplish and one that is meaningful to you.

Goal 6: Write goals down and put them where you can see them every day. Goals will not do you any good if you do not remember them. For this reason, experts advise that you write your goals down and keep them where you can see them every day. They are not meant to be a taunt but a motivator about what you want to accomplish. If you see your goals every day, you will know immediately if you are achieving them or not.

Goal 7: Make goals performance oriented not outcome oriented. As noted earlier, do not make goals that concern tasks or accomplishments that you cannot control. For example, if you set a goal of winning a trophy on the track team, you cannot control all the other runners. You can only control yourself. You can work and practice and lift weights, but another runner still may be faster than you.

However, if your goals are based on your performance, then you can control what happens. In this case, you might have a goal of lifting weights 3 days a week and doing cardiovascular training 2 days a week while also practicing with the track team. This goal takes into account the things that you can control in your environment.

## The Resources

The following resources offer more information about the specifics of setting and tracking your goals:

*http://Webnz.co.nz/checkers/GoalSetting.html*

This Website offers excellent steps to help you set goals and motivate yourself to study.

*http://Webnz.co.nz/checkers/settinggoals2.html*

Here, the same Website offers forms to help you set goals and keep them.

*www.siue.edu/SPIN/activity.html*

This Website by The National Association for Developmental Education offers a list of effective goal-setting techniques for college students.

# 1

# Avoiding Procrastination

A part-time college student has an essay due tomorrow morning, and she has not started it yet. She has to work until closing at her job and will not get home until 11 p.m. She is so worried about the grade her paper will earn that she cannot concentrate and complete even the outline before she goes to work.

Because she has waited until the last minute, she is sure that she will fail the paper and the class. She is too embarrassed to ask her friends or family for help. She is thinking about calling in sick to work, but she needs the money to pay for school. She thinks that maybe she should just drop out of school because she will probably fail anyway.

Instead of working on her paper, she spends her time feeling anxious, worried about her grades and angry with herself. She needs to find a more effective way to deal with her schoolwork.

## The Challenge

Psychologists believe that most people procrastinate. One study estimated that at least 90 percent of college students occasionally procrastinate on their schoolwork. Of these, experts think that about 25 percent have a habit of procrastinating on all of their assignments. These chronic procrastinators are usually the students who drop out of school.

Procrastination is the process of avoiding a task that you have agreed to accomplish. Although many procrastinators seem calm on the outside, most feel guilty and even depressed about not completing their work on time. A habit of procrastination can cause students a great deal of difficulty in school and can cause even worse problems in later life.

Writing a paper at the last minute may get you through school, but if you continue to turn your work in late to a boss or supervisor, you could be fired or demoted. The most successful students and those who accomplish the most on the job overcome the urge to procrastinate.

## The Facts

Most students procrastinate for more than one reason, which makes it difficult to change the habit. Following are the five main reasons that students procrastinate:

1. Unrealistic Expectations.

    Some students expect to accomplish huge tasks. For example, students with unrealistic expectations may believe that they have to read everything about a subject before they can present a speech on that topic. A more realistic expectation would be to check three or four sources and then choose the main points for the speech.

2. Fear of Failure.

    Some students avoid completing a project because they are afraid that they will receive a bad grade. By not writing the paper at all, the student never has to find out. For example, some people procrastinate because they feel that they are failures if they do not get an A on every assignment. These students think that their grades equal their self-worth.

3. Perfectionism.

    Perfectionism is a belief that you must meet the very highest standards of accomplishment and not make any mistakes. Students who are perfectionists often believe that if they fail a test or do poorly on a paper, the grade represents their worth as human beings. They believe that they are good people if they get good grades and bad people if they do poorly.

4. Difficulty Concentrating.

    Students who procrastinate often have trouble concentrating on their work. They daydream when they should be studying and talk with nearby students instead of starting their projects. For example, such a student might stare at a picture of his girlfriend instead of starting his English paper.

5. Scheduling Problems.

    Procrastinators frequently do not manage their time well. They feel that they cannot control their own time or that it gets away from them. They may feel overwhelmed by a project or paper and worry about it instead of doing it. These students may clean their apartments, run errands and offer to help other family members instead of doing their own work.

## The Solutions

The best way to quit procrastinating is to realize that this habit is not making your life easier. On the contrary, it is making your life more difficult and could ruin your college career or job opportunities. It is a myth that most people do their best work at the last minute. Very few students can write an A-quality essay an hour or two before it is due.

You need to begin earlier and plan better. Following are six tips to help you accomplish your goals on time without waiting until the last minute:

Tip 1: Small, Specific Goals.

Big projects such as a research paper, a group presentation or an essay can be scary. Instead of focusing on the whole project, divide it into steps. Make each step into small, specific goals. For example, do not plan to study every night for a week. Plan to study from 3:30 to 5:30 p.m. on Monday, Wednesday and Friday and from 5:30 to 7:30 p.m. on Tuesday and Thursday. It is easier to accomplish small, specific goals such as making an outline, reading one chapter or finding five research sources than it is to write an essay, read a 100-page assignment or create a research project.

Tip 2: Instant Rewards.

Reward yourself for accomplishing the specific tasks that you have set for yourself. For example, after you have read one chapter of a textbook and drafted an outline for your essay, spend time with friends, play a video game or watch your favorite television program. Rewarding yourself will help you complete the small, specific tasks that make up the big projects.

Tip 3: Good Work Space.

Figure out where you get the most work done. For example, some students study better at home. Others can concentrate better in a quiet library or study hall. A few students can write better in places such as coffee shops or restaurants where they can tune out everything else. Find out which location is the best for you. Once you know where you work best, plan to spend the bulk of your study time in these locations.

Tip 4: Realistic Task Estimation.

Some procrastinators are not good at figuring out how long a task will take. For example, they underestimate the amount of time it will take to read two chapters in a textbook, write an essay or prepare a speech. Because they underestimate the time that their studying will take, they do not give themselves enough time to accomplish their work. If this is your problem, start by doubling your time estimates. If you think it will take 1 hour to read a chapter, give yourself 2 hours to complete the task. Then, note the amount of time it actually took and adjust your estimate in the future.

Tip 5: Short Sessions.

If you procrastinate, begin by working for short sessions. Do something concrete to show yourself that you are working toward your overall goal. Do not overtax yourself or you may begin to daydream. If you create specific tasks, complete them in short bursts and immediately reward yourself, you are setting a healthy pattern of achieving your goals. For example, give yourself an hour to come up with an outline for your essay. Create a thesis statement and then list your main points. Under the main points, list the specific examples for each point. Create a topic sentence for your concluding paragraph. If you create a pattern of success, you will be more likely to continue doing your work rather than procrastinating.

Tip 6: Getting Started.

Many procrastinators have problems getting started on their work. For example, they cannot decide what topic to write about for an essay, so they do not do the essay at all. If this is your problem, remember that you can always edit or change your essay once you have it down on paper or in a computer. Instead of trying to make it perfect, just get it done. No matter how terrible the first draft is, you can always rewrite or rethink it. It is much easier to rewrite an essay than to try to write it from scratch.

## The Resources

The following resources offer more information about the specifics of avoiding procrastination:

*www.salisbury.edu/students/counseling/New/Procrastination_Assess.htm*

This Website contains a quiz to help you determine if you are a habitual procrastinator.

*www.cla.purdue.edu/asc/resources/overcoming_procrastination.pdf*

This .pdf document from Purdue University offers a good problem solving process for changing your habits to be more productive.

*www.studygs.net/attmot3.htm*

This Website offers more useful tips to help you build better work and study habits.

*www.academic.udayton.edu/legal/online/study/procra01.htm*

This Website contains a seven-step program to help you change your habit of procrastination forever.

*www.cla.purdue.edu/asc/resources/perfectionism.pdf*

If you suspect that you are a perfectionist, print this .pdf document from Purdue University. The article offers examples of unrealistic and realistic goal setting.

*www.salisbury.edu/counseling/asp.htm*

This Website offers excellent suggestions to break the cycle of procrastination.

# 2

# Scheduling Your Time

A middle-aged professional woman has been out of school for a long time. She is concerned that she will not do as well in her classes as the younger students. She is rusty at studying and did not work very hard the last time she was in school.

She knows that now she will take school more seriously, but she is worried that she will not be able to do the work, get good grades and complete a degree. In particular, she is afraid of failing. She also does not want to be the oldest person in the classroom besides the teacher and is worried that she will not fit in.

Because she has a family, she is concerned about managing her time. She wants to give herself enough time to study and take care of her children and husband. She hopes that she can juggle all of her commitments successfully.

## The Challenge

The challenge for students is managing their time effectively so that they have time to do their schoolwork, take care of personal responsibilities and get together with friends and family. The difficulty is spending the appropriate number of hours studying while also fitting in personal tasks such as laundry, errands, jobs, eating, sleeping and going to class. The best students also manage to have a little time leftover to spend with friends and family.

## The Facts

Every student has the same number of hours each week. Some students manage to fit everything they need to do into those hours while others feel that they never have enough time. The difference between the two is how they manage their time. With practice and patience, any student can learn to manage his or her time effectively.

### Time Audit

First, you need to figure out how well you use your time already. The best way to do this is to fill out a time audit form. The Resources section of this chapter lists several Websites that will help you.

One site automatically adds up all the hours you spend in a week based on information that you provide. Another includes information about how many classes you are taking and what grade you want to earn in each class.

A time audit will help you figure out the following:

- Number of hours of sleep each night;
- number of hours for showering and grooming;
- number of hours spent commuting, including parking and walking;
- number of hours spent going to organized activities such as church, clubs, sports, etc.;
- number of hours spent at a job; and
- number of hours spent with family and friends for relaxation.

Multiplying these daily totals by seven gives you the total number of hours you use up in a week. Subtract this number from 168–the total number of hours in a week–to find out how much time is left in your schedule for studying.

Study experts advise students to spend 2 hours studying for every hour spent in class. For most students, that means 8 to 10 hours per week of studying. Completing papers and projects will require more time. Do you have enough time in your current schedule to study? If not, what can you do to find more time?

## Planning

Scheduling your time depends heavily on planning. Students need to have long-term and short-term plans to help them manage their time effectively.

Long-term planning should include a master schedule or semester/quarter schedule. This schedule lists all scheduled tests, quizzes, papers, projects, speeches, etc. that your teachers have assigned. In most classes, teachers pass out a syllabus during the first week that includes every assignment. All of these required projects can go on the master schedule.

In addition, students can add all of their personal and family commitments and obligations. Add the dates for spring break, winter holiday break, days off school and any job information that you know in advance. This should give you a good overview of what you need to do for the semester.

Short-term planning involves creating both monthly and weekly schedules. Some students also like to create a daily plan. The more planning you do, the easier your life will be and the more you will feel in control of your time.

Monthly schedules should include such things as papers, projects or tests listed on the master schedule. In addition, students can add their family or personal obligations such as church, clubs, jobs and other responsibilities. Students also should include their study times.

A weekly schedule lists reading and project assignments due for the week, regular church or club obligations, the study schedule and the schedule for paid work. Students can look at this schedule and see what is required for the week.

If students opt for a daily schedule, they usually use an index card to list the five or six items that need to be accomplished for the day. Many students list their actual study times on this card as well as their work hours.

## The Solutions

Learning to manage your time and create good schedules for yourself is a skill that will pay dividends throughout your life. No matter what your career, you will be faced with a large number of things that need to get done in a limited amount of time. Being able to manage your time efficiently will make you a more valuable employee and manager.

The key to time management is doing the most important tasks first. People who teach strategies to save money have a saying: Pay yourself first. What they mean is that if you want to save money, you need to put away your savings first and then live on the rest of your income. If saving money is your priority, this is what you should do first.

The same can be said of studying. Put studying at the top of your list of things to do. If you wait to study until all of your other obligations have been fulfilled, you will never find enough time to do it properly.

The following time management tips will help you keep to your schedule:

Break large tasks into smaller pieces.
> Writing a research paper is a daunting task. However, if you break this big project down into its various constituent parts, you will have an easier time accomplishing the task.

Try to study every day.
> Doing well on a test depends on feeling confident. If you study a little every day, you will feel good about taking the test. If you cram for hours the night before, you will be even more worried about how you will do.

Use the time between classes to study.
> There is no rule that you have to study for hours every day. You can fit your studying into spare minutes during the day. Study between classes, during lunch and when you are waiting in lines. Many students make flash cards that they carry with them. When you are waiting in line, go over the flashcards to help you memorize key concepts or vocabulary.

Reward yourself for sticking to your schedule.

Make sure that you allow yourself a reward for staying with your schedule. Spend time with friends, watch television or just relax. You will find it easier to keep to your schedule if you acknowledge your successes and reward yourself.

Factor in some extra time for flexibility.

Very few things go the way we expect, so add some extra time into your schedule for those unforeseen emergencies. If you have an extra half-hour built into your schedule, you will not be worried if you have to stay an extra half-hour at work or get caught in traffic.

Just do it.

Some students are so worried about doing their assignments perfectly that they cannot get the assignments completed. Being able to turn in the assignment at the proper time is the most important thing. Teachers seldom give points for late work.

Say no.

Keep your priorities in mind when people ask you to volunteer for activities or your friends want to go out. Feel free to say no. Write your priorities on an index card and keep it with you to remind you. Going to class is first, studying is second, personal obligations are third and spending time with friends is fourth.

## The Resources

The following resources offer more information about the specifics of time management:

*www.ucc.vt.edu/stdysk/TMinteractive.html*

You can find an automated time audit document here to help you figure out how you use your time now. This interactive program automatically adds up all the hours you spend in a week based on information that you provide.

*http://studytips.aac.ohiou.edu/?Function=TimeMgt&Type=168hour*

This Website offers an excellent interactive time management program from Ohio University.

*www.dartmouth.edu/%7Eacskills/success/time.html*

For monthly, weekly and master schedule blanks and more time management tips, check out this useful Website from Dartmouth College.

*www.how-to-study.com/Keeping%20Track%20of%20Assignmentsprint.htm*

This Website includes many good tips for managing your time and keeping track of assignments.

# Motivating Yourself

A first-year university student is having trouble finding time to study and do his homework. He knows that he needs to spend more time studying because his classes are the hardest he has ever had. Unfortunately, he waits until he feels like studying, and he is not often in the mood.

Sometimes he gets angry because his teachers talk fast and cover so much material in every class. He is expected to read at least 100 pages a week in his textbook and write a response paper to what he has read; and that is just for one class. With four classes, he is overwhelmed by the workload. He feels that no one can do this much work in a week and suspects that the other students are not completing their assignments either.

He would like his professors to go slower and assign fewer chapters every week. He thinks only one class a week should assign a paper so he would not have to write two or three. Almost every day, he wakes up at 3 a.m. in a panic thinking that he will flunk out of school and disappoint his parents.

## The Challenge

Motivating yourself to study can be difficult. In fact, most students have trouble with motivation from time to time. The best students know why they are in school in the first place and are internally motivated to succeed. But even students who are serious about school can have a bad attitude about studying.

Most students learn to cope with their study patterns and find ways to motivate themselves when they are tired, stressed or overworked. The trick is to find your own inner motivation. Once you understand what you want from the situation, you can find interesting information in even the most difficult subjects.

## The Facts

Challenging yourself and your attitude can be an occasional or a chronic problem for students. The key is the student's motivation to go to school. Students who are deeply dedicated can sometimes have a bad day or find a particular class or teacher troublesome. However, individuals who are not motivated to attend school or have not thought about their motivation can find themselves in an unending spiral of anger and fear.

If you seldom feel like studying and often feel angry with your teachers, the other students or anyone who urged you to go to school, you may need to rethink your priorities, goals and motivation.

Ask yourself the following questions:

Why are you in school?

This may seem like an obvious question, but many students have never asked themselves this basic question. The answer is very important. Students who are in school because it is expected of them, because their parents wanted them to go or because all their friends were going may find it difficult to be successful because their motivation comes from outside themselves. They are working to please someone else. The most successful students know why they are in school, and they want to be there for their own reasons. They are motivated by their inner desires.

What career are you interested in?

Some students are interesting in attaining knowledge for its own sake. However, most students have a vested interest in going to school because they have a specific career in mind, and they have to earn a degree to enter that career. Students who are uninterested in their classes or find them boring often can improve their motivation by choosing a career and working towards the goal of entering that field. Students should ask themselves what kind of job they want when they finish school. What are they interested in or passionate about? Many students take a variety of classes during their first few years in order to find a subject or career that interests them. Identifying subjects that students find boring or difficult can help them narrow their choices.

What is your major and why did you choose it?

Students who are motivated to do well in school usually have chosen a major and know why they are studying in that field. Students who choose a major because of their parents' wishes are much less motivated to do well. Inner motivation—also called self-directed motivation—is selfish in a good way. Self-directed people understand how they will benefit from going to school, so they study and complete assignments even when they do not feel like it. Students who are motivated by other people or outside forces are less likely to overcome their own procrastination or fears.

Are you angry?

Students who do not choose their own path are often angry with others.

They blame their professors, the other students or the educational system for their difficulties studying, completing assignments and being successful in school. Because their motivation does not come from within, they have little reason to do what is expected of them. They may feel justified in procrastinating on their assignments or completing them late because the system, the subject or the professor are all against them. Self-motivated students understand what they will gain from their education, so they work hard.

Are you afraid of success or failure?

Some students are afraid of failing at school, and some may be even more afraid of succeeding. Success in school means that others–parents, future bosses and friends–will expect even more of them. Success in school may make students think that they have to get a job, buy a house and start a family immediately after they graduate. Some of them see themselves growing up too fast. Many students do not want to recreate their parents' life, but feel a great pressure to do so. Self-motivated students know that they make their own choices in life and will continue to move forward at their own pace.

## The Solutions

Unlike many other study topics, motivation is deep and complicated. The solutions are not easy, but students can find their own motivation and become successful if they answer the questions above honestly and follow the four motivation tips below:

1. In the beginning, look at effort rather than results.

    Do not look at how much you accomplish. Instead, concentrate on all the effort you are expending to reach your goal. For example, do not focus on how many chapters you have read but on how much time you have blocked out to do your reading. If you put in sincere effort, you ultimately will have excellent results.

2. Adjust your expectations and be realistic.

    If you have been neglecting your studies, do not expect to catch up in a week or two. Adjust your expectations to something more realistic. Do not remind yourself of what you should have done. Instead, set reasonable goals for what you will accomplish. Do not try to do too much too fast. If you push yourself too hard, you will lose your motivation very quickly. Remember that it takes time to build good habits and that you are working towards your goals.

3. Monitor your internal dialogue.

    What kinds of message do you give yourself during the day? Do you say,

*I can do this*, or do you say *I am no good at school; I should quit*. Remember to congratulate yourself when you study and complete your assignments. When you think of something negative about yourself, stop immediately. Do not allow negative thoughts to go through your mind. Being positive and upbeat starts with you. Treat yourself as well as you treat your friends. Remind yourself of all the good things you have done and that you are working towards your goals.

4. Take charge of your own learning.

The key to self-motivation is to take charge of your own learning. Remember that you are responsible for your success in life. Your professors, parents and friends can help you, but the choices are yours to make. Figure out how you learn best and create lessons to help you understand and remember the concepts you learn in class. Get a tutor or go to the tutoring center at your school. Create a study group. Do something to help yourself learn the materials more quickly and more completely. Your success or failure in school is up to you.

## The Resources

The following resources offer more information about the specifics of motivating yourself to do schoolwork:

*http://vcs.ccc.cccd.edu/crs/star/educ120/intro2EL.htm#Key*

This Website discusses the key characteristics of excellent students. It demonstrates how the very best students take charge of their own learning.

*www.dartmouth.edu/%7Eacskills/success/study.html*

This concise Website from Dartmouth College offers everything you need to know about motivation.

*www.twu.edu/o-sl/counseling/SelfHelp041.html*

This Website from the Texas Woman's University is all about finding your inner motivation.

# Rewarding Yourself

A part-time graduate student is feeling burned out. Because she was worried about not doing as well as the younger students, she has studied nonstop for weeks. She has completed all of her assignments early, but she is not spending any time with her family. Although she feels better about school, she is beginning to worry that she is neglecting them. She wants to spend time with her family, but she is worried that she will fall behind in her classes.

## The Challenge

Achieving balance in life is a common goal. In particular, students have a difficult time managing all of their responsibilities and their schedules. Studying too much can burn you out and make it even more difficult to prepare for examinations and projects at the end of the term. Smart students learn to pace themselves and reward themselves.

Rewarding yourself for completing your schoolwork or studying is not just a treat. You need to rest sometimes so that you can conserve your strength. You need to be able to recharge your batteries, think about something besides school and relax. Rest is critical to being a successful student.

That is why achieving a workable balance between schoolwork, relaxation and home life is so important for students. The other areas of your life can help you relax and also can bolster your self-esteem and motivation.

## The Facts

Many students do not understand that rewards are a necessary part of the study process. If you give yourself occasional breaks and rewards, you will be more likely to stick to your study schedule, complete your assignments on time and feel good about your accomplishments.

To be successful, you need to remember these three facts about the schoolwork/ rewards process:

1. Study is hard work.

Studying, taking tests, writing papers, giving speeches and creating projects are all difficult, time-consuming tasks. You may find it helpful to look at being a student as though it were your job. Most people spend at least 8 hours at their workplace every day. Are you spending the appropriate number of hours doing your job as a student? If so, you need to reward yourself with an appropriate amount of downtime and recreation.

2. Study first; play later.

The best way to complete your schoolwork in a timely fashion and create a school/life balance is to study first. After your work is done, you can relax and play. If you organize your life around this simple mantra, you will be able to avoid guilt, procrastination, anger and self-doubt.

Trying to do too much too soon is a recipe for disaster—If you ignore your needs for rest and relaxation, you will burn yourself out. The human body and mind are only meant to work for so long before they require rest. This is why most experts advise people to sleep for at least 8 hours per night. Our bodies need to rest and regenerate so that we can work hard. Students who try to push themselves for a long period of time will regret it. Their minds and bodies will not be able to deal with the strain. They may become ill or be unable to concentrate for more than a few minutes at a time. Schedule your work and play time and reward yourself immediately for completing the schedule.

3. You can train yourself to study.

You have probably heard of Professor Pavlov's dog. Pavlov was a scientist who was studying conditioning. Every day when he fed his dog, he rang a bell and then put the food dish into the dog's cage. After a while, the dog would expect to be fed every time the bell rang. Even if Pavlov did not bring the food every time the bell rang, the dog still expected to get fed. You can condition yourself in much the same way. Reward yourself every time that you complete your work. After a short while, you will want to do the work in order to get the reward.

## The Solutions

If you want to succeed as a student, you need to find appropriate rewards for yourself. You will need various levels of rewards to account for the various levels of schoolwork. For example, if you are scheduled to complete an outline for your paper, read a chapter in history and study for a math test, you might give yourself a 10-minute break after you completed the outline and another after you read your history chapter.

However, once you were done studying for the math test, you might want to give yourself a bigger reward because you completed everything on your schedule. You might treat yourself to a snack, go and get a pizza with friends or take time to watch your favorite television show. It is important that the rewards be significant to you.

The following list includes some other options for rewarding yourself:

Choose rewards that have meaning for you.

Think about rewards that you would really like. Part of the motivation for getting your work done is enjoying the reward, so make it something that you would look forward to doing. Rewards are different for everybody. For example, while the graduate student might enjoy spending time with her family or helping her children complete their homework, many other students would not consider spending time with family to be a reward.

Make a list.

It may seem obvious or silly, but make a list of the rewards that you want. For example, you may reward yourself with dinner out after you complete the first draft of your English paper. On the other hand, you may allow yourself to get a snack when you complete the research for your paper and only give yourself a break when you complete the outline. To be most effective, the reward needs to correspond to the difficulty of the task you completed. Finishing pieces of a larger project should earn you larger rewards.

Create rewards that are readily available.

If Pavlov had promised to give his dog an extra special dinner in a week if the dog got excited at the bell today, the experiment would not have been successful. As human animals, we work best when our rewards are immediate. The cause and effect of doing work and getting a reward helps to keep you motivated to do more work. Remember to choose items that you have on hand.

Choose rewards that are relatively inexpensive.

The reason to do this is so that you can provide both lesser and greater rewards for yourself. The biggest rewards can cost the most money. For example, you may decide to give yourself a special spring break trip because you improved your grade in astronomy.

Choose rewards that are everyday luxuries.

Think of things that you might buy for a friend or relative. If you like cologne or aftershave, make a special trip to buy some as a reward. If you have to save money for school, reward yourself with a dinner out when you complete your speech project on time. If you are watching your weight, choose a special chocolate reward, a new item of clothing or some music downloads as rewards for something that you find especially difficult. For example, you might allow yourself to buy a favorite candy bar or expensive clothing item if you did not procrastinate about studying for your statistics test.

Remember to correlate the reward with the effort that you expended. Giving yourself a reward for getting a good grade can be self-defeating. If the subject is very difficult for you, you need to reward yourself for studying, getting a tutor and improving your grade not for earning a C. Take yourself to a movie, have coffee with a friend or read a favorite non-school book.

If you are short on cash, think of rewards that cost nothing.

You can study your hardest subject—or your least favorite one—first and then reward yourself by studying the subject you like best. You can do the same thing with reading assignments or any other kind of assignment. Do the hardest work at the beginning of your study period when you will be the most refreshed and energetic. Tackle your easier subjects later when you will be more tired.

## The Resources

The following resources offer more information about the specifics of creating good rewards for yourself:

*www.learningassistance.com*

Click on Student Sudy Skills Tips. This area gives you plenty of ideas about rewards for yourself and why rewarding yourself is the best way to encourage good study habits.

*www.d.umn.edu/psychology/online_courses/study.html*

This Website from the psychology department of the University of Minnesota at Duluth offers helpful insight into training yourself to study on a regular basis.

*www.sbcc.cc.ca.us/learningresources/Website/orientation/skills/motiv.htm*

This Website includes tips for motivating yourself and creating workable goals for schoolwork.

# 5

# Studying
# Distractions

## The Challenge

A junior-high student was only interested in the social aspects of school. As far as she was concerned, the classes were just annoying interruptions to her social life. She never really gave her future much thought.

One day, she realized that she did not have any goals beyond having fun, and she wanted more in her future. Suddenly, school became important, but this student realized that she did not know how to study, take tests or succeed in academics.

## The Facts

Research has shown that some students study better with music playing in the background while others require complete silence to be able to concentrate. You need to decide what distractions bother you and which you can tune out.

To succeed at studying and become a good student, you need to make sure that you can minimize all or most of the following distractions:

- Background noise such as:
    - television
    - radio
    - cell phone
    - computer
    - music

You need to be able to concentrate on your work and not be distracted by outside noises, especially when you first sit down to study. These noises remind you of all the other things you could be doing instead of studying.

- Visual distractions such as:
    - computer
    - television
    - art work
    - light too bright
    - light too dim

Some people are more distracted by images than by sounds. If this is true of you, you need to make sure that your study space is free of visual distractions. For most people, the only distractions would be things directly in their line of sight.

- People interruptions such as:
  - friends stopping to talk to you
  - people walking by
  - people around you talking

Most students report that the biggest impediment to their studying is their friends. If you have friends who are serious students, you may be able to study together and both get work done. However, most friends may end up talking about things that are not related to studying and distract you.

- Break issues such as:
  - taking too few or too many breaks
  - taking breaks that are too long

Many students make one of two mistakes about studying. Some do not take a break at all and try to study for hours. Others take frequent breaks that get longer and longer. Successful students need to find a balance between giving themselves a short rest and getting back to work.

- Physical annoyances such as:
  - too cold
  - too hot
  - uncomfortable chair
  - table or desk wrong size or height

Every student is different, so you need to adjust yourself to your study environment. If you are too warm, you will get sleepy and find it difficult to concentrate. If you are too cold, you will be uncomfortable and also find it difficult to concentrate. Similarly, you must be comfortable with the desk and chair you are using. Find out, for example, if you concentrate better at a single-person desk or at a bigger library table.

- Personal issues such as:
  - thinking about significant other
  - thinking about parents
  - thinking about friends
  - worrying about schoolwork
  - worrying about tests
  - worrying about grades
  - feeling sick

Students cannot do their best work if they are concerned about extracurricular problems. Experts advise students to put their other problems on hold while they study. This can be difficult to do if students are worrying specifically about their schoolwork or grades. Students who are sick should consider putting their studying off. Research shows that students cannot do their best work when they are physically ill.

- Assignment problems such as:
  - did not bring the right textbook
  - did not bring the right notebook
  - did not bring the right equipment to study
  - did not write down the assignment

All of the study time in the world will not help you if you bring the wrong textbook or do not write down the appropriate assignments. Experts advise that students bring more than one study assignment with them in case they finish the first assignment early or bring the wrong materials.

## The Solutions

The best way to minimize distractions is to deal with them before they come up.

### Background Noise

Turn off the television, radio and your cell phone. Disable the instant messaging function on your computer or turn it off completely. If you are in a study space where you cannot turn off the ambient noise, bring along an MP3 player and listen to it on headphones.

### Visual Distractions

If the blinking screen on your computer or the screensaver is distracting to you, turn the computer off. Turn off the television. If this is not possible, sit with your back to the distraction and wear headphones. Adjust the light to the level that works best for what you are doing.

### People Interruptions

You do not have to put up with friends who disturb you while you are studying, and you do not have to be rude. By turning off your cell phone—including the text messaging function—and instant messaging function on your computer, you are allowing your friends to contact you, but you do not need to respond to them immediately. As soon as you are done studying, you can check your e-mail and messages.

### Break Issues

When you are studying, you need to take breaks. Research about concentration indicates that students can study for 1 to 1.5 hours before they need a break. If you are studying complex subjects such as math or science, you may need a break more often.

### Physical Distractions

If your study space is too hot or too cold, wear layers so that you can adjust your body temperature as needed. Experts advise that students cannot study if they are uncomfortable with the temperature. In addition, choose a chair or desk that is the right size and height for you to do your reading and writing. You want a flat space big enough to hold all of your books and papers.

### Personal Problems

Psychologists suggest that students put their personal and family problems in a box when they sit down to study. Imagine all the people you are worried about or who are annoying you being put into a box. The problems cannot get out of the box until you let them out. If the problems seem to escape, imagine yourself securing the lid or putting a weight on top of it. Now you can study without worrying about them. Remind yourself that you can pick up your worries again after you are done. Turning your cell phone off also will help.

### Assignment Problems

The best way to keep track of assignments is to write down each assignment as you get it. Keep all your school assignments in the same notebook. If you have a personal digital assistant (PDA), keep all your assignments in there. Make sure to back up your PDA on a regular basis, or you may lose the information.

While you are studying, you can keep a pad of paper at hand. When you think of something you need to do, just jot it down. This way, you will not forget what you need to do, but it will not disturb your study time.

## The Resources

The following resources offer more information about the specifics of minimizing or avoiding distractions:

*http://guts.studentorg.wisc.edu/SS/newsshandbk2006.htm#Quiz*

This study skills quiz is a good way to find out about your study habits. If your score indicates that you need to work on various study skills, you can read the appropriate chapter in this book.

*www.salisbury.edu/students/counseling/asp.html*

Click on How good are my study skills? Take this assessment to find out how good your study skills are. Tally your score to find out what you need to work on.

# 6

# Setting Up a Study Space

A successful student never spent much time studying, and he always did pretty well in school. Then one day everything changed. Now, the reading seems endless and the tests impossible to pass. This student really has to work just to get a passing grade. Since he wants to graduate, he knows that he needs to become a better student and that means studying.

Unfortunately, he already has many bad habits to break. He watches television while he studies, does his homework at the last minute and e-mails his friends while he should be reading his assignments. If he gets 5 hours of sleep a night, he feels he is doing well.

While he studies in his room, his desk is piled high with his laptop computer, his MP3 player, a set of speakers and a laundry basket filled with clean clothes. Even if he puts the clothes away, there is no room on his desk to study. His friends constantly call him or send messages, and they usually want him to go out instead of studying.

## The Challenge

The first step to becoming a good student is to set up a workable study environment. While some students may swear that they can study in front of the television, with their MP3 player on full blast or sitting at a table with other students, research shows that most students do their most efficient studying in a quiet environment.

Studying, like most every other human activity, can be done efficiently and effectively, and this skill can be taught. Hours and hours of ineffective study cannot make up for not studying. Studying all day or all night to catch up on a subject and do well on the test is not an effective or efficient way to get a good grade.

The best way to do well on a test is to study every day and every week on a schedule. Studying each subject for just 20 minutes a day is more efficient than studying any one subject the entire weekend before the test.

If you manage your time well, you also can include time in your schedule for fun activities, work, family obligations and everything else in your busy life.

## The Facts

A study space needs to have all of the following qualities in order to be useful:

- The space needs to be available whenever you need or want to study. Studies show that 80 percent of study time for most students is spent at home and not in a study hall or library. Create a space at home that you can use whenever you need to study.

- The space needs a table or desk that is big enough to hold all of your reference materials, schoolbooks, paper, pens and even a computer. Unless you want to be searching for the appropriate list, pen or notebook every few minutes, you need a study space that is big enough to hold all of your study materials or a study space with storage. You can store materials such as a thesaurus, dictionary or encyclopedia until you need them.

- The space needs to have a reasonably comfortable chair. If your chair is too comfortable, you may find yourself becoming sleepy. On the other hand, you can permanently injure your back by sitting in a chair that is uncomfortable. Choose a chair that is comfortable enough to sit in for several hours at a time.

- The space needs good lighting that you can adjust as necessary. You need to be able to read your textbooks, take notes and stay awake during your study time. For this reason, you need an adjustable light. During daylight hours, you may not need the light or may only need to set it on its lowest setting. In the evening or late at night, you may want to turn the light up to its highest setting to help boost your attention and concentration.

- The space needs a moderate temperature that you can control to some extent. As you know from sitting in a classroom, a space that is too warm can cause you to feel sleepy. A space that is too cold will have you concentrating on your shivering instead of your work. You want a space where you at least can open a window if you are feeling too warm. If you study late at night or early in the morning, opening a window may help you concentrate.

- The space needs to be quiet or have a door that you can close when you are studying. As noted earlier, most people really do concentrate better in a quiet room. Even if you are sure that you can handle the noise, try a quiet room for a while to see how easy it is to concentrate. Make sure that your family, roommates and friends all know your study schedule so that you will not be interrupted. Turn off your cell phone and disable the instant messaging feature on your computer during your study time.

- The space needs to be a place where you only study. For a variety of reasons that will be explained later, you need to study in a space that you do not use for anything else. For example, you can study at the desk in your room and move somewhere else in your room to call your friends, play video games or eat snacks.

## The Solutions

There is both a mental and a physical aspect to studying. You probably already know that you can physically be sitting in a nice, quiet place and still not feel like studying. For this reason, you want to associate your study location with the act of studying. It may seem obvious or foolish, but writers and other professionals understand the importance of symbols and ritual to your attitude and behavior.

For example, some professional writers swear that they feel like writing the minute they sit down at their writing desk or computer. This is because they have trained themselves to write when they are sitting in a particular space. In that space, they have a mental habit of doing the same thing over and over again—in this case writing—so they automatically start thinking about it the instant they sit down.

You can do the same thing with your study space. If you sit down and study in your space over and over again, you will find that you automatically start thinking about the latest chapter you read, the last lecture you attended or the probable questions on the next test.

Some researchers suggest that students wear a particular item of clothing or set a particular symbolic item on their desk when they are studying. This will help to ensure that your subconscious mind understands that when you are physically in your study spot, you need to be mentally ready to study.

## The Resources

The following resources offer more information about the specifics of setting up a good spot for study:

*www.ucs.umn.edu/lasc/handouts/lascpdf/studyhabit.pdf*

This Website includes an excellent study skills inventory to help you focus on what may be keeping you from successful studying.

*www.how-to-study.com/Preparing to Study.htm*

*www.howtostudy.com* is a good place for general study information, including how to set up your study space, how to prevent distractions and how to tackle difficult books, papers or projects.

*www.ucc.vt.edu/stdysk/concentr.html*
*www.ucc.vt.edu/stdysk/control.html*

> These two Virginia Tech Websites offer specific guidelines about concentration and controlling your study environment.

*www.adprima.com/studyout.htm*

> This article about how to study is a useful overview for those just beginning to take their studying seriously.

*www.childdevelopmentinfo.com/learning/studytips.shtml*

> This Website can help parents figure out how to set up a good study space. It is also an excellent resource if your parents, siblings or roommates interrupt your study time. Send them to this site so that they can check out the study etiquette rules.

*http://memory.learninginfo.org/study_habits_tips.htm*

> This clear and concise article can help anyone overcome his or her fears about studying.

*www.girlslife.com/oct04/quizstudy.php*

> Here is a useful study quiz from Girls Life magazine. Both girls and boys can benefit from finding out their study scores based on this quiz.

# 7

# M.U.R.D.E.R. Study Systems & Classroom Tips for Success

An eighth-grade student is having trouble in her history class, and she has not made a good impression on the teacher. She sits in the back of the classroom near the window and periodically looks out at the students walking by. She has her notebook in front of her and a pen in her hand, but she does not take many notes.

She does not understand how to be successful in this class. She reads the assignments but cannot seem to remember them very well during tests; she needs a way to look at her materials and organize them so that she can succeed.

## The Challenge

Most students have difficulty concentrating in classes they find difficult or dull. They need a method for thinking about and organizing the materials that will help them do well on the tests. One such method is a study technique called M.U.R.D.E.R.

In addition, although teachers work very hard to treat all students equally, they can misunderstand a student's outward demeanor. For example, a student who sits in the front of the room, takes notes and makes eye contact with the teacher likely will be perceived as being enthusiastic about and interested in the class.

On the other hand, a student who sits in the last row or near the window, does not seem to be taking notes and looks out the window from time to time can be seen as being disinterested. Teachers are much more likely to give extra help and study advice to the former student because he or she seems to be engaged in the class. Teachers are less likely to provide help to students whom they perceive as being bored or indifferent to the material.

## The Facts

The M.U.R.D.E.R. study system uses a mnemonic device to help students remember it. Each letter in M.U.R.D.E.R. stands for a step in the process. Because the word murder applied to academic study sounds ridiculous, it is easier for students to recall.

The following is an explanation of the six-step process:

M = Mood

In order to study successfully, you need to set a positive mood for yourself. This mood should include your study space and personal attitude. A good attitude and a quiet environment can make studying much easier.

U = Understand

While you are reading, note the information that you do not understand. You can do this by highlighting the section, using a sticky note or writing down the page numbers on a notepad.

R = Recall

After you have finished reading or studying the section or unit that you are working on, stop and recall what you learned. Put the information into your own words as if you were explaining it to a friend.

D = Digest

Go back to the sections that you marked because you did not understand them. Look at the information again. If you still do not understand it, find an explanation. You can try asking your teacher, looking on the Internet or finding another book on the subject.

E = Expand

Ask yourself three types of questions about what you have just learned. First, what kinds of questions would you ask if you could talk directly to the author? Do you have criticisms or other comments for the author? Second, can you make the material apply to your own life and the things that interest you? Third, what do you need to do to make this information easier for other students to understand?

R = Review

Consider the ways that you have tried to remember information or concepts in the past. What methods worked for you? Can you apply these methods to the current material?

## The Solutions

Once you have mastered the M.U.R.D.E.R. study system or another technique, you are halfway to becoming a successful student. The other half of your success depends upon your behavior in class. Some classes are held in huge lecture halls where the professor has teaching assistants to help teach the class. Others are held in small classrooms with 20 to 40 desks. No matter how many students are in your class, you need to consider carefully how you present yourself.

To that end, the following are 10 tips to help you succeed in the classroom:

1. Sit in front.

    From the front of the room, you can see the chalkboard or view the screen clearly and hear the professor with little effort.

2. Listen and take notes.

    While this may seem obvious, in any class you can see a number of students who are doing neither. Taking notes alerts the teacher that you care about what he or she is saying. In addition, your notes serve as a reminder of the lecture so that you can study for tests.

3. Ask questions.

    In a large lecture hall, many students do not want to draw attention to themselves by asking a question. If you are nervous about asking a question, go to your teacher and ask your question before or after class. Asking questions alerts the teacher that you care enough about the class to want to understand the concepts.

4. Participate in discussions.

    Teachers take note of which students join the class discussions. In most cases, the brightest students are the ones who feel confident enough to speak up. No matter how you feel about yourself, you need to participate. Speaking up once or twice a week is enough to show the teacher that you are engaged in the subject and the class.

5. Do not argue with or complain to the teacher.

    The best way to put a teacher on the defensive is to argue with him or her about a grade. This is the worst possible way to gain the teacher's attention. The second worst way is to go to the teacher to complain about something. If you have questions about how an assignment was graded or exactly what the teacher was looking for, ask him or her in private. Find out how you can improve your grade on the next project.

6. Be on time to class.

    Teachers notice which students come in late. In fact, some teachers consider it a sign of disrespect for students to come late to class. It is as if the student is saying that the class is not important enough to bother about being on time.

7. Write out all assignments clearly or use a computer.

    These days, most teachers ask that submitted work be processed on a computer. However, on essay tests and response papers, students are allowed to write their assignments by hand. Make sure that your handwriting is neat and clear. The teacher will be reading many papers. Make his or her life easier by writing neatly. Research has shown that neatly handwritten assignments often are given higher grades.

8. Turn in all assignments on time.

Another way to bring yourself to the teacher's notice in a bad way is to turn in your assignments late. Many teachers will not accept late work, and some teachers consider it rude to hand in work after it is due. Students who turn in late work can be perceived to be too busy or uninterested to do the assignment.

9. Do all the homework.

Teachers take note of who always does the homework and who does not. Doing the homework is a good way for you to get practice in the subject area and find out what the teacher is looking for in assignments. Find out what the teacher wants before you have to turn in a big assignment for a big grade.

10. Do not let others distract you.

Do not look out the window or toward the door if someone comes in late. Do not use your cell phone, listen to your MP3 player or send e-mail. Listen and focus on the professor so that you will get all of the information. Teachers generally ask more questions about their in-class lectures than they do about the assigned reading.

## The Resources

The following resources offer more information about classroom tips and the M.U.R.D.E.R. study system:

*www.educatingjane.com/Study/MURDER.htm*

Primarily aimed at smart girls, this Website has a good explanation of the M.U.R.D.E.R. study system and a variety of other study-related information.

*www.studygs.net/attmot2.htm*

This Website offers excellent suggestions for influencing teachers. Although the information is adapted from the famous *How to Win Friends and Influence People* by Dale Carnegie, everything here is good advice.

*www.studygs.net/metacognition.htm*

This Website offers interesting information about learning how to learn. Visit this site if you want to know more about yourself and how you learn things.

# 8

# Do Your Homework

A college student is having difficulty with his history class. The class is held in a large lecture hall with over 300 students. The professor lectures every class and gives large reading assignments. The lectures do not contain any pictures, slides or PowerPoint® presentations.

They never discuss the reading in class, so the student does not know if he understands the material well or not. While he understands the lectures well enough, he has not been turning in the homework assignments to the professor's teaching assistant (TA).

The homework does not count toward his grade, but the TA does keep track of it. Most weeks, the student is supposed to write a reaction paper to the assigned reading. He thinks that the assignment is just busywork, so he has not done it. However, the TA will be grading the in-class essay exam at the end of the semester.

## The Challenge

Many students have difficulties doing their homework. Some students think that the assignments are only busywork. Others have trouble doing all the reading, let alone extra assignments. No matter the reason, homework is usually helpful to the student.

Homework accomplishes two things. First, it helps the student to practice using the material learned in class. Students write papers about the reading or practice math problems or discuss poetry, so they have a chance to use what they have learned. Second, homework helps students understand what the teacher is looking for in class assignments.

For a number of students, homework is difficult because of the student's preferred learning style. According to education experts, all students learn in a variety of ways. However, each person has one specific way that is the easiest for him or her. The goal for students is to find their preferred learning style and gear all their study efforts toward that style.

## The Facts

A variety of experts have divided the ways students learn into different profiles or systems. One popular method is called the preferred learning style. According to this system, students learn in one of the three following ways:

1. Auditory

   Auditory learners learn best by listening. They do well in classes with teacher lectures, class discussion and verbal repetition of materials. For this reason, many auditory learners are good at learning foreign languages. Auditory learners also can learn better by listening to audiotapes, talking to someone else about what they have learned or reading their textbooks aloud.

2. Visual

   Visual learners learn best by seeing. They do well in classes that use pictures, diagrams and written outlines or lecture notes. They usually do well when the professor writes on a chalkboard, uses an overhead projector or provides outline notes for each lecture. Visual learners also can learn by taking detailed notes during lectures, visualizing concepts and remembering lists with mnemonic devices.

3. Kinesthetic/Tactile

   Kinesthetic/tactile learners learn best by doing. They do well in classes where they need to physically handle samples, equipment or devices. They do best in a classroom with a lab requirement. This type of learner also can learn by handling the actual objects discussed in the class, doing experiments or by creating movement-oriented memorization techniques.

Students can learn in all three ways, but one method will come most naturally. The best students try to figure out their preferred learning style and use that information to help them study, write papers, create projects and review for tests.

## The Solutions

Even the best students can benefit from tips to help them do their homework more efficiently. Following are 10 tips to help students work smarter:

Tip 1: Write down the assignment.

   This may seem obvious, but few students actually do it. Writing down each assignment in each class is the best way to make sure that you know what to do. If you think that you will remember what was required, you may be surprised to find that you cannot remember if it was Chapter 11 or Chapter 21 that you were supposed to read for the quiz on Thursday. If you write everything down, you never have to worry.

Tip 2: Ask questions.

If you do not understand the assignment, ask the teacher about it. If you are shy or nervous, ask the teacher before or after class. You can ask the teacher how long the assignment should take or what he or she expects for the assignment. Asking questions shows the teacher that you care about the class.

Tip 3: Start your homework in school.

If possible, start your homework while you are still at school. Use the time between classes, at lunch or before and after class to begin your homework. This is a good practice because you can have any questions answered before you go home. In addition, the more work you do in the afternoon, the less you have to do in the evening.

Tip 4: Prioritize.

Look at your homework for the night and figure out what you need to do first. Experts advise that you do your most difficult subject–or the subject you are least interested in–first and save your easiest subjects for the end of the evening. Also, look at when the assignments are due. Complete the ones that are due soonest first. For example, you may decide that since you have basketball practice tonight, you will complete the outline of your history paper first and then read your English homework after practice.

Tip 5: Budget your time.

After you prioritize your work, estimate how much time it will take you to complete it. Be sure to add extra time for your hardest classes. Make sure that you complete the highest priority assignments first and that you spend most of your budgeted time on them. After they are completed, you can begin homework that is easier or has a lower priority.

Tip 6: Do the hardest work first.

Start your homework period by working on your toughest assignment. This usually will be the first priority anyway. Easier tasks can be accomplished later in the evening. You want to tackle your toughest class or assignment when your energy level is highest and that is at the beginning of your study or homework time.

Tip 7: Do not obsess about the work you have to do; just do it.

Many students get into a pattern of worrying about their homework but not doing it. Instead of waiting until you can make your homework perfect, just get it done. By its very nature, homework is something that you do every day or most days. Because of this, you can risk turning in one or two imperfect assignments. The two most important facets of homework are doing it and turning it in on time.

Tip 8: Put completed assignments away immediately.

As soon as you have finished a homework assignment, put it in your school bag for the next day. Waiting to put all your assignments away at the same time provides opportunity for something bad to happen to your work or for you to forget it. If this happens, you will not earn credit for the work you have completed.

Tip 9: If you do not understand, ask for help immediately.

If you do not understand the homework assignment once you get home, do it anyway. Do your best, but ask the teacher to help you the next day. If your teacher is too busy or unapproachable, ask another teacher who teaches the same subject, your parents, another student or a tutor. Do not allow yourself to fall behind in class.

Tip 10: Reward yourself.

After you have completed your homework, reward yourself. Watch a movie, talk with friends or eat your favorite snacks. In fact, some students visualize their reward before they begin doing their homework to motivate themselves. You deserve a break and to have fun.

## The Resources

The following resources offer more information about homework tips and learning styles:

*www.ncsu.edu/felder-public/ILSpage.html*

This Website developed by Richard M. Felder and Barbara A. Soloman of North Carolina State University offers an online quiz to help students figure out how they learn best. The site also offers information about learning styles and a comprehensive discussion of how each type of learner can improve.

*www.advisorteam.org/instruments*

This Website offers an online personality test that uses information from the Myers-Briggs Type Indicator. It also offers explanations of the various personality types and can help students to understand themselves better.

*www.accelerated-learning.net/multiple.htm*

This Website offers an interesting definition of the multiple intelligences that Harvard's professor Howard Gardner has created and offers a test that students can print out. This site is useful for students who want to find out their learning strengths.

*http://kidshealth.org/teen/school_jobs/school/homework.html*

This Website offers many homework tips.

# *9* Prioritize

A junior in high school has recently decided to become a better student. While she does not know exactly how, she has decided to begin by doing all of her homework every night. Unfortunately, she sometimes has to stay up late to get everything done.

When she does not get enough sleep, she finds that she cannot concentrate well in class and does not take very good notes. She would like to organize her studying and homework better and figure out how to prioritize her work.

Currently, she does her assignments in random order. Sometimes she does not get finished until 1 a.m. She knows that there must be a better way to do her work, but she does not know what it is.

## The Challenge

The problem for many students is that they cannot figure out how to organize their work in order of importance. Some spend all of their time doing the projects that are due soonest and do not work on those that are due later. Some do all of their other homework first and then have to stay up late to complete the work that is due the next day.

Organizing any project is just a matter of looking at all the pertinent information and deciding the order in which items should be completed. Ordering the items on a list according to their priority is one of the most useful skills that students can learn.

In addition, prioritizing is also useful in the work world. The most successful entrepreneurs, business leaders, authors and teachers use priority lists to make their lives and their businesses run more smoothly.

## The Facts

Even the most successful business leaders cannot do everything at once. The best approach to any project is to complete one item and then move on to the next one. Students can achieve success by prioritizing their assignments and then completing them in order of their importance.

This method is successful because it requires people to do all of the following:

- Get projects accomplished.

    Prioritizing helps to keep students organized. Being organized helps them to do their work and complete their assignments on time. Getting projects such as term papers, research projects and speech presentations done in a timely fashion is the best possible reason to prioritize your work.

- Feel less stressed.

    Students who have prioritized their tasks feel less stressed because they have a plan. They do not worry about how they will accomplish their goals–they know. The plan helps them to relax and concentrate.

- Say no.

    Most students have more things to do than they have time to do them. For this reason, students need to learn to say no to other responsibilities, projects or assignments that are not required for school. If you know what you need to do and when you need to do it, you can explain to others that your time is already committed.

- Schedule time for sleeping and eating.

    If you already have a plan to complete all of your work, you can then plan sufficient time to sleep, eat and relax. Students cannot study, memorize or plan their schoolwork if they are not appropriately rested.

- Sort out the difference between urgent and important.

    Because students have too much to do and too little time to do it, they need to prioritize their work and the rest of their lives. Once their lives are organized and prioritized, they can look at all their responsibilities and decide which are important and which are only urgent.

Just because something is urgent does not mean that you have to do it immediately. Perhaps you are not the one with the urgent need. Maybe your roommate or friend urgently needs you to do something. You need to ask yourself if this activity is important. It may be of supreme importance to your roommate or friend, but is it important to you and your school priorities?

Your schoolwork may have to come first, especially at the end of the term. Perhaps your friend can call someone else for help or borrow your car without you in it. If you have your priorities organized appropriately, you will be able to look at every request for your time and decide if it is genuinely important or just urgent.

## The Solutions

Many students do not know how to prioritize their work. They can create a schedule, but they have difficulty deciding which projects should come first. A priority list is not merely a to-do list. It is a list that numbers all of the things you need to do in order of importance.

Use the following steps to prioritize your schoolwork, your life or your business:

Step 1: Check the due dates for all of your projects.

Prioritizing requires students to gather a wide variety of information and make decisions based on that data. The first thing you need to know is when your assignments are due. You can create priorities for a day, a week, a month or the semester, but you first need to know when everything is due.

Step 2: Estimate the time required to complete each assignment.

Once you know all your due dates, look at each project and estimate how long it will take you to complete each one. Feel free to break larger projects into smaller steps. In addition, add some extra time just in case your estimates are off. Many things are outside of your control. You may need to wait in line to gain access to materials, have a difficult time finding a quiet place to study or need to buy a printer ribbon at the last minute. If you have estimated too much time, you will just finish your work early. If you estimated too little time, you will cause yourself excess stress.

Step 3: Think about the time available to complete the work.

When you know the due dates and have estimated the time needed to complete the work, you need to consider the time that you have available. Think about any paid work that you need to do and any church or family responsibilities that you have already committed to do. Concentrate on figuring out how to organize all the work.

Step 4: Consider your study skills and talents.

Next, you need to look at yourself. Which assignments are easy for you? Which are more difficult? Experts advise students to tackle their most difficult assignments—or the assignments that they are least interested in— at the beginning of their study time or when they are most alert. Difficult tasks will take more time and will require your peak concentration.

Step 5: Consider your most productive times.

Finally, figure out your most productive times to do schoolwork. Are you an early riser? Are you a night owl? Do you need coffee before you can concentrate on any difficult task? You need to think about the times that you are able to concentrate best and schedule your most difficult assignments during this time. Easier tasks or things that you are naturally good at can wait until you have time to complete them.

Step 6: Make a list and ask yourself the following questions.

By now, you should have a good list of everything that you have to do and all the things you will need to get them done. Make sure that you have listed everything you need to do, even the smaller pieces of the big projects.

Before you assign numbers to any of these items, ask yourself the following questions:

- What do I need to do now?
- What can I schedule for later?
- What can I get others to do?
- What can I put off until later?

Once you have answered these questions, you can begin to add numbers to your work list. Assign numbers to everything on the list and decide which items you will accomplish each day.

## The Resources

The following resources offer more information about setting priorities:

*www.academictips.org/acad/timemanagement.html*

This excellent Website offers students a number of study tips, but it also provides especially good tips on prioritizing schoolwork.

*www.studygs.net/timman.htm*

This Website's section on time management covers all the steps needed to prioritize your work.

*www.law.ttu.edu/lawWeb/oasp/tips/TipsForSuccessDuringExams.shtm*

This Website from the Texas Tech University School of Law is especially useful for deciding what you need to know before setting the priority of your work. This site also contains advice on exam preparation.

# *10*

# Remembering

A freshman at college is having a hard time studying for her next round of tests. She knows that she needs to review her notes and prepare for the tests, but she does not know what to do. When she sits down, she just stares at her notes. She reads through them over and over again, but she does not feel as if she remembers very much of what she reads.

As the tests draw near, she is concerned that she will not do well because she does not have the right skills to study and remember all the material. The more worried she becomes, the more her stress level rises. She wishes that she knew more about being a good student.

## The Challenge

Remembering key information from classes is one of a student's main jobs. Besides writing papers, creating projects and presenting speeches, students also spend a great deal of time preparing for and taking tests. From short quizzes to lengthy final examinations, students need to know how to study for tests in order to be successful in school.

## The Facts

Experts have divided memorization into two types: general and rote. Students use general memorization when they are asked to remember general information and main concepts about a subject and to put these concepts into their own words. Rote memorization occurs when students are required to remember specific information about a subject, such as definitions, facts, dates and formulas, and to write down or recognize the exact wording on a test.

Many students find it difficult to memorize large amounts of information and to access that information during a test. In order to do this, you must move the information from your brain's short-term memory into its long-term memory. Research shows, however, that people do not retain very much of what they try to remember. According to experts, a great deal of learned information is gone after just 5 minutes. Approximately two-thirds of the information is gone in 1 hour. After a whole day, 90 percent of what you worked so hard to remember is gone.

However, you can remember large amounts of information for much longer if you can move that information into your long-term memory. With training and practice, students can greatly improve their memorization skills.

Long ago, students were asked to memorize famous speeches, poems and other important documents. Although many of them learned this information when they were in grade school, they could still remember most of the literature even into old age.

If you learned to recite Lincoln's Gettysburg Address–Fourscore and 7 years ago… or the Longfellow poem Song of Hiawatha–By the shores of Gitche Gumee, By the shining, Big-Sea-Water…in grade school, you will likely take those famous words with you wherever you go. If you can remember information from all those years ago, you can remember the subjects that you are studying now.

## The Solutions

Once you learn to move information from short-term to long-term memory, you will not have trouble studying for examinations. Following are some tips to help students learn to memorize general information such as concepts, main ideas and theories and put this information into their own words:

### Relax

Students learn best when they are relaxed. Allowing yourself to feel stressed about your tests or studying will not make it easier to memorize the appropriate information. Experts also advise students to get enough sleep when they are studying. Students learn less efficiently when they are tired and worried.

### Believe

Studying and memorization are about believing in yourself. If you believe that you can remember all the information for your test and do well, you will be able to do so. On the other hand, if you are worried that you cannot learn everything before your test, you will not remember the information. In many ways, students are what they believe they are. Good students know this and feel confident because of their past academic success.

### Focus

Research has demonstrated that the mere fact that you want to remember information will help you to do so. Look carefully at the information you want to remember and repeat it in your mind. Concentrate only on what you need to remember and do not worry about anything else.

## Associate

One of the best ways to remember something is to associate it with something that you already know. Information that you already know is stored in your long-term memory. Associating–sometimes called attaching–the new information with old information will help you to remember more effectively. For example, if you already know about the Romantic poets from your English class, you could associate information about that same period from your history class with the information that you already know.

## Exaggerate

Another trick to help you remember information is to exaggerate an image or create a humorous jingle about the information. For example, if you need to remember the exact date that Columbus came to America, you could use the old rhyme–Columbus sailed the ocean blue in 1492. In more recent times, a children's television program created funny music and words to help people remember such things as how a bill becomes a law–I'm just a bill on Capital Hill–and how conjunctions work–Conjunction Junction, what's your function?

You can do the same thing by imagining a tyrannosaurus singing and dancing if you need to know the names of periods of the Stone Age. You also can create a jingle, rhyme or rap about the periodic tables, the order of the American presidents or anything else that you have to know for a test. The more outrageous or funny your song or image, the easier it will be to remember the information.

## Visualize and Use Your Senses

Visualizing the information that you need to remember is even more efficient if you can use your senses in the image you create. Your five senses can make it easier for you to remember information. The more senses that you can put into your image, the better you will remember the information. Smell is especially helpful to memory. If you need to remember the periodic table, try to come up with smells, tastes, sights and sounds for each element.

## Chunk

Divide a large memorization task into smaller pieces. This way, you can learn smaller bits of information and then chunk them together into a whole. For example, if you have to memorize the periodic table, you can divide the whole table into pieces–gases, solids, liquids, etc.–and learn each section separately. Then you can chunk all the information together, and you will know the whole table.

## Read Aloud

All students can benefit from reading their notes aloud. If you are an auditory learner, this method may be the one that you want to use most of the time. Auditory learners learn best if they talk about what they are learning or repeat it aloud. Use your hearing to help you remember.

### Review and Repeat

While it may seem obvious, memorization researchers have proved that reviewing your notes over and over again for just a few minutes at a time is a good way to remember them. Reviewing for hours just before the exam–also called cramming–is not a useful technique. However, reviewing the main points of each chapter for just a few minutes several times a day for a week or more is a very good method to move data from your short-term into your long-term memory.

### Understand

Information that students understand is much easier for them to remember. Thoroughly understanding the theories, concepts and main ideas that you are trying to memorize will help you do a better job of remembering. In fact, understanding the concept first is the best way to learn new material.

### Overlearn

Overlearning is the process of studying for more time than you think you will need just to be sure that you are prepared for a test. Research has shown that studying for 50 percent more time than you think you will need can yield as much as 50 percent better memory retention. In fact, if you overlearn 50 percent, experiments prove that you will remember six times as much as you would have if you crammed for the test.

## The Resources

The following resources offer more information about memorization techniques:

*www.sas.calpoly.edu/asc/ssl/memorization.html*

This Website from California Polytechnic State University offers plenty of facts and data about how the brain remembers and how students can use this information to improve their own memory.

*www.ucc.vt.edu/stdysk/remember.html*

This Website from Virginia Tech offers over 15 tips to help students memorize better.

*www.studentzona.com/2005/11/08/memorizing-tips/*

This Website offers a variety of study materials for students and some excellent advice about how to improve memory without wasting time.

# 11

# Rote
# Memorization

A premed student is taking a science class, and he is struggling. He needs to memorize all the types of rocks for his geology course, and he does not think he can do it. Although he still has 2 weeks before the test, he is already concerned about his grade.

He needs to do well on this test in order to get a B for the semester. Unfortunately, he has not spent much time studying yet. He is thinking about the best way to remember all these names, but he has not had much practice at memorizing long lists of information.

## The Challenge

Rote memorization, the verbatim remembering of a list of facts, dates, chemicals or other data, has been out of fashion since the 1970s. Despite hundreds of years of education using this method exclusively, most grade school teachers do not consider rote memorization a useful learning tool for children.

Because of this educational trend, most college-aged students seldom have been asked to memorize anything more complicated than the multiplication tables. Since they did not get much practice with memorization in elementary school, many students have problems learning to memorize information in high school and college.

Unfortunately, when called upon to memorize a large amount of information, many students do not know where to begin.

## The Facts

As noted in the preceding chapter, there are two types of memorization: general and rote. Rote memorization is the process of remembering the exact wording of a sentence, phrase or list of information. This type of memorization usually is required in the sciences, engineering, math, foreign languages and theater.

Although it has been disproved by research, most students believe that cram sessions–all-night studying of the material for a test–are useful. In truth, cram sessions do not help students remember well, and they cause students a great deal of stress and worry.

In fact, learning experts have known for a long time that the best way to practice rote memorization is to divide the process into 5 to 10-minute stretches. Students spend these short blocks of time reviewing information that they need to be able to recall for the test.

Students can use notecards, notebook paper, a PDA or a computer to list the information that they need to know. All they have to do is go over the material a number of times a day for just a few minutes.

## The Solutions

The following method of rote memorization works better than hours and hours of study over time or an overnight cram session just before the test. However, many students may not want to bother with reviewing the information three to six times a day. Those students should consider the following facts:

- The more we recall a piece of information from our mind, the better we remember it. The number of times that you recall something you have learned can help to move that information into your long-term memory.

- When information is in your long-term memory, it does not go away. Under normal circumstances, you can recall it at any time.

- The human brain is made up of billions of nerve cells which are joined together in a complex web that forms memories. Students want to take up as many nerve cells as possible with the information they will need for their tests.

Research indicates that students who use the following method of rote memorization remember more in a shorter amount of time than those who study for hours. This method is also called distributed learning.

- Learn information to be memorized.
  First, learn the information that you must know exactly. Try to keep the list fairly short. Experts advise that most people remember the first and last items on a list the best and have more trouble recalling the middle.

- Five minutes later, take a few minutes to review the information again.
  Do not allow yourself to be distracted or disturbed. Repeat the information over to yourself again until you have it all correct. Many students find it easy to write their list on an index card and carry it around with them for review. If possible, repeat the information aloud.

- One hour later, take a few minutes to review the information again.
  Find a quiet place such as the library, your car or your room. Repeat the information over to yourself again. In fact, say it aloud to yourself. If the list of information does not have to be in a specific order, feel free to put it in an order that sounds good to you. If possible, try to create a word order that rhymes or is singsong.

Research has shown that rhymes, singsong and poems are easier for people to remember than plain lists of information. If the list has to be in a specific order, try to make a silly song out of the words. The funnier the song, the easier it will be to remember. In addition, a funny or silly song will make you laugh, and that will help you relax during the test.

- Three hours later, review the information again.
  Repeat the whole thing again. Once is enough, but feel free to repeat the information over and over. The more you do it, the easier it will be to remember the next time you need to review it. Saying or singing it aloud is best, but you also can repeat it to yourself under your breath or go over the list in your head.

- Six hours later, review the information again.
  Repeat the information again. Think of it as a mantra for your test. Once is good. Three or four times are better. Repetition is the key to moving this data from your short-term memory into your long-term memory.

- Review the information before bed.
  Studies have shown that just before bed is a good time to practice memorization techniques. Because most people are relaxed before bed, their brains are especially receptive to information. In fact, reviewing index cards, notes for a presentation or anything that you need to remember just before going to sleep is a great way to memorize information with very little effort.

- Review the information three times during the next day.
  Practice reviewing the information at least three times during the day after you memorized the information for the first time. Choose three times evenly spaced throughout your day. Repeating the information three times in a row will not provide much help. The more you repeat the information over time, the more you will remember it.

- Review the information three times during the third day.
  On the second day after you learned the material, you will need to repeat the information again three times. Intersperse the review periods throughout your day so that a few hours go by between each session. Each review session should take just a few minutes to complete.

Considering all the repetitions, this method of rote memorization should take the average student about 40 minutes to do for each list of information. If, for example, a student must memorize the periodic table or some complicated math formulas, the larger list needs to be broken into smaller sub-lists. Once the student learns each sub-list using this method, he or she can chunk all the lists together and practice them.

By breaking the larger memorization task into smaller ones, a student can memorize almost any amount of information and keep it in his or her long-term memory.

## The Resources

The following resources offer more information about how to memorize information by rote:

*www.studyhall.com/MEM/memory.html*

This Website offers a variety of study tools, including a list of tips for improving memory. It provides general memorization tips and then explains three different methods for memorizing large lists of data.

*www.maexamhelp.com/study_cards.htm*

This Website is geared toward students in a medical assisting program, but their advice about memorization is excellent. Since medical assistants must memorize huge lists of medical terms, their techniques for studying and memorizing are first-rate.

*www.vyomworld.com/memory/rote_memorization_using_repetition.asp*

This Website explains how repetition is the key to rote memorization. It also discusses how to create notecards to aid recall.

*www.fit.edu/caps/articles/documents/!MEMORYT.pdf*

This Website offers 20 extremely useful tips to help students memorize any kind of information. The authors, Douglas Mason and Mike Kohn, are considered to be experts in the field of learning skills and memorization.

*www.ebtx.com/math/rotemem.htm*

This essay explains the rationale behind using rote memorization in math classes. In addition, the author advocates rote memorization for most subjects in grade school, high school and college.

# 12

# Using Index Cards to Study

A new graduate student is getting ready for her final examinations, and she is stressed. She seems to carry all of her books wherever she goes. She began studying and reviewing every subject about 3 weeks ago, but she is not confident that she will pass all her exams.

She wishes that there was a simple way to review all of her class materials without having to drag every book around with her. Although she is trying to use every spare minute to study, she feels that she does not have enough time.

When she does not have her books with her, she carries all her notes and tries to sift through the pages. Although she highlights the important sections, it still amounts to five or six notebooks.

## The Challenge

Even for students who are motivated, studying for chapter tests and midterm exams can be a chore. Reading through all of your notes and rereading the textbook can be difficult if you are trying to finish up major projects for other classes.

Some students use computers to make their studying easier. They do their note taking on computer and then organize the notes by key word. However, this process can be lengthy and tiresome. In addition, typing the information does not have the same effect as writing it out. Some experts advise students to take notes by hand because the kinesthetic process of writing helps students to remember the concepts.

One time-tested method of studying for tests and examinations is called index card studying, also known as flashcard studying. As the name implies, students carry index cards with them to help them study.

## The Facts

Index card studying is a simple process that can be used for any course material or subject. The following list includes everything students need to know about this method of study:

Use notecards.

> Purchase some index cards, also called notecards. Some students prefer 3-by-5 cards while others like the larger format of 4-by-6 cards. Colored cards also work well. You also can cut regular pieces of paper to the same size, but they will be difficult to shuffle. In addition, you can see the answer through the paper, which defeats the purpose.

Write a question on one side.

> Write a question on one side of the card. The question can be about a definition, a concept, a method, a theory, a formula–anything you need to study for class.

Write the answer to the question on the other side.

> Answer the question on the other side of the card. If you are required to memorize a specific formula or answer, use the exact words or figures that you need to know. If you just need to understand a concept or theory, you can use your own words or a shorthand version.

Mix the cards up.

> Shuffle the cards well so that you will not remember which answers go with which questions. If you fail to mix the cards up adequately, you run the risk of memorizing the information in a particular order. You may not be able to explain the material if the test questions are in a different order.

Go through the stack and try to answer the questions.

> Read the question on each card and try to answer it aloud. You may want to do this in your car or apartment so that it does not appear that you are talking to yourself. After you answer the question, verify the answer on the back of the card.

Create a stack for the questions that you know.

> If you provided the correct answer to the question, place the card in a stack in front of you. You will be making two piles, so remember which stack is which.

Create a stack for the questions that you do not know.

> If you did not answer the question correctly, place the card on the other stack. If you did get the answer, but you do not feel that you know the material well enough, put the card in this pile.

After you have gone through the entire stack, shuffle the cards that you do not know again.

Go through the cards that you did not answer correctly one more time. Make two stacks as before. Go through the questions you do not answer correctly again until you have answered every one.

Review the cards often during the days leading up to the test.
Take your stack of cards with you. Shuffle them carefully and go through them whenever you have a few spare minutes—for example, if you are waiting in line, waiting for an appointment, between classes or even at lunch. This method is highly effective, and it requires just a few minutes throughout the day.

## The Solutions

While the index card method is easy, it can be difficult to figure out what to put on each card. The following tips will help you to create excellent flashcards that you can carry around with you easily:

Do not use more than 200 cards at a time.
No matter what size cards you decide to use, do not create more than about 200 of them. More than that can be difficult to memorize and transport. For the midterm or final examination, you can study the cards containing the main ideas of each chapter.

Use index cards to learn definitions, lists, dates and facts.
If your class requires you to memorize hundreds of new terms, put one term on each index card is an ideal way to learn them. This method also works for lists and facts that you have to remember.

Use index cards for potential essay questions.
Try to second-guess what the teacher will put on the test or exam. Think about what you have learned and think of an appropriate essay question for the teacher to ask. Use shorthand or just the key terms for the answer. Do not attempt to write or memorize an essay answer. If you know the key points, you will be able to write a good essay.

Use index cards for other questions you think will be on the test.
Think about other types of questions—multiple-choice, true/false, short answer—that you might ask if you were the teacher. This kind of thinking is very helpful. If you get good at it, you can study more appropriately.

Use index cards for general concepts, theories or movements.
Sometimes students do not need to memorize exact wording, figures or dates. Instead, they need to know the main points about a concept, a theory or a historical movement.

Use index cards for points that your teacher mentioned two or three times.
One good way to figure out what will be on the test is to think about concepts, ideas, movements or theories that your teacher mentioned more than once in class. If the teacher took the time to mention a point more than once, it is probably important.

Use index cards for points that your textbook covers at length.
Another good way to anticipate test questions is to look carefully at your textbook. What concepts, ideas and theories does the textbook spend the most time on? Teachers often ask questions about issues that the textbook covered in-depth.

Review your index cards by yourself, with your study group or with a study partner.
The index card method works equally well for individuals, study groups or study partners. However, the more different methods that you use to study, the better prepared you will be for the test.

## The Resources

The following resources offer more information about the index card study method:

*www.accd.edu/sac/slac/handouts/Studyaids/sskills_aid_7.htm*

This handout from San Antonio College provides an excellent assortment of tips about creating and using flashcards.

*www.bookrags.com/articles/26.html*

This Website offers a wide variety of study materials. The section about using notecards to memorize material is very useful.

*www.studygs.net/tstprp4.htm*

This Website offers a one-page summary about how to use index cards to succeed in school.

# 13

# Improve Your
# Listening Skills

A college student is sitting in his philosophy class and listening to his MP3 player. He tried to listen to the professor for the first hour, but the man is wearing two different colored socks and has six different-sized buttons on his shirt. The student decides that anyone who cannot dress himself in the morning probably does not know anything interesting.

Besides, the student does not agree with what the teacher is saying. The girl next to him has the same opinion. The two share their MP3 players until class is over and then go out for coffee.

## The Challenge

Paying attention in class can be difficult. In addition to dealing with the instructor's speech pattern and idiosyncrasies, students also must take notes, deal with distractions and adjust to the temperature and lighting of the room. Most students manage to accomplish this.

However, some students do not understand the subtle difference between listening and hearing. While they may hear the instructor, they will not do well in the class unless they listen carefully.

## The Facts

Some students do not understand how to listen. Unfortunately, most classes in college involve lectures by the instructor, a teaching assistant or even the students themselves. Students can help themselves succeed in school by avoiding the following habits of bad listeners:

- Making fun of the speaker.
  Bad listeners look for almost any excuse to stop paying attention. Often, they spend the whole lecture making fun of the way the teacher dresses, the teacher's speech pattern or the teacher's mannerisms. While they are doing this, they completely miss everything that the teacher has said.

- Thinking the subject is boring without even listening.

  Students often make decisions about classes based on what other students say or on the impression they form after the first class. Unfortunately, many students do not pay attention to the teacher because they consider the topic boring. Whether it is or not, the student still needs to be successful on the test.

- Disagreeing with the speaker.

  Bad listeners allow themselves to get upset if the teacher challenges any of their beliefs. Once these students are angry, they stop listening or taking notes.

- Getting distracted.

  Many bad listeners are just easily distracted. They are more interested in what their classmates are doing than in what the teacher is saying. Some students leave their cell phones on so that they can send text messages to their friends.

- Trying to write down everything the speaker says.

  Some bad listeners are trying diligently to pay attention, but they are paying attention to the wrong things. These students try to write down everything that the speaker says instead of the main points. Every single detail of the teacher's lecture will not be on the test, only the main points. Students who try to write everything down may miss the key issues being discussed.

- Daydreaming if the material is too complicated.

  Some bad listeners do not want to work very hard. If the teacher talks about complicated topics or complex theories, they get frustrated and refuse to listen further. Some of these students do not want to learn anything new or are worried that they cannot comprehend high-level topics.

- Failing to use time to their advantage.

  Experts estimate that the average speaker can talk at a rate of approximately 100 words per minute. However, the average listener can think at a rate of 400 words per minute. Bad listeners fail to use this ratio to their advantage. These students often drift in and out of the lecture instead of using the time effectively to take good notes.

## The Solutions

Even the worst of bad listeners can learn to do better. Listening is a skill that can be learned just as studying, reading and writing can. With a little practice and some effort, any student can become an excellent listener by using the following tips:

Come prepared to take notes.

Come to class with all the appropriate materials to take notes and a good attitude. If you choose to do so, you can find something interesting in any subject. If you do, you will do a better job of listening and taking notes. If all else fails, remember that you are paying for this class. As a good consumer, you want to get your money's worth from the professor.

Sit in front.

Sit where you can hear and see the speaker. Do not sit near friends or roommates because they may distract you. Put away anything that does not directly pertain to taking notes. Sitting in front is also a good way to impress the teacher. Teachers take note of students who always sit in the front row. Many instructors automatically think that those in the front are the brightest and the most interested in the subject area.

Listen for clues to the main points.

Most speakers give verbal clues as to the organization of their material. They will say such things as first, next, secondly, in addition to or the main point is, this will be on the test, the most important feature is. No matter how disorganized a speaker may be, he or she will alert you to the main points. Some speakers mark them verbally, while others make physical gestures. If you watch the teacher carefully, you will not have any difficulty figuring out the main points of the lecture.

Think of questions as you are listening.

Keep yourself involved in the lecture by thinking of questions you would like to have answered by the end. This exercise will make you an independent learner instead of a passive listener. You can jot these questions down as long as they do not interrupt your note taking.

Try to anticipate the speaker's next point.

Another way to keep yourself involved in the lecture is to anticipate the teacher's next point. If the subject is of interest to you, you should be able to figure out the structure of the speech from the first main point or two. Remember that you are only paraphrasing the instructor. You do not need to write down everything he or she says. As noted earlier, you can think four times faster than the speaker can speak. Use this time to take good notes.

Do not judge based on appearances.

College professors may dress oddly, speak strangely and have very little interest in what students think of them. However, they are teachers because they are interested in a subject and want to share it with others. No matter how silly the teacher looks or acts, try to concentrate on what he or she is saying. Most professors are experts in their field, and many of them are fascinating human beings.

Keep an open mind.

College is a time for students to learn new ideas, concepts and theories. Many of these theories may be very different from what they have learned previously. College should teach students to have an open mind. Do not dismiss an idea because your parents are opposed to it. Look at the idea from every viewpoint, and decide what you think about it. College is an opportunity for you to look at many different ideas and choose which ones you will believe in.

## The Resources

The following resources offer more information about listening skills:

*http://home.snu.edu/~hculbert/listen.htm*

This Website from Southern Nazarene University offers good tips about paying attention and taking effective notes during a lecture. In addition, this site has an excellent range of other study skills topics.

*http://dl.clackamas.cc.or.us/os11class/LearningSkills/listenskills.htm*

This information from Clackamas Community College offers excellent insight into how the brain functions when listening. The sidebar Dendrite Connection is especially useful.

*www.scs.tamu.edu/selfhelp/elibrary/listening_skills.asp*

This Website from Texas A & M University includes very practical advice about listening to lectures. The list of tips for students in the classroom is impressive.

*www.uiowa.edu/web/advisingcenter/aac_curr_students/improving/note%20taking.htm*

This Website from the University of Iowa offers information about taking notes, editing notes and listening to lectures. All three areas are covered thoroughly on this site.

# Taking Notes in Class

A promising college student is having trouble keeping up in his philosophy class. His teacher speaks very quickly, so he is having difficulty writing down everything that she says. Each class, he uses up at least one pen and dozens of sheets of paper in his notebook.

He sees that the other students are not writing as much as he is, but he does not know how to take fewer notes. He does not want to miss anything that the teacher says. He finds that he is writing down the questions that the other students ask as well as the teacher's answers.

The student knows that there must be a better way to take notes, but he does not know how to find it.

## The Challenge

In high school and college, students need to take notes so they can succeed. However, many students have never taken a study skills class and do not know exactly how to take classroom notes in an organized fashion.

Most students just write as fast as they can and invent shorthand symbols and abbreviations for themselves. Unfortunately, when they are ready to study for a test, some students forget what they meant by their abbreviations and symbols. These students spend a great deal of time trying to decipher their notes in addition to studying for the test.

Students need to know how to take notes in an organized fashion and be able to understand those notes later.

## The Facts

Many students take notes without really understanding why they are doing so. They see that everyone else is taking notes and that the teacher expects them to, so they do. However, there are a number of excellent reasons to take notes besides peer and teacher pressure. Following are eight reasons why students need to take notes in class:

1. Identify the main points in the teacher's lecture.

   One of the best reasons for students to take notes is so that they can identify the main points the teacher makes in his or her lectures. Some teachers are very organized and will lecture as if from an outline. These teachers make it easy for their students to take notes. However, many instructors do not use this method and may seem to lecture randomly as students ask questions. Students need to keep accurate notes for both kinds of teachers.

2. Help remember information for the test.

   Another excellent reason to go to class and take notes is that you will need the information for the test. Some teachers offer review sheets for their tests, but most do not. For this reason, students need to keep accurate notes so that they can use them as study guides for the test.

3. Only chance to learn information not in the book.

   Unless the teacher is also the author of the textbook, most teachers use the text as an ancillary to their lectures. This means that the textbook is not as important as the teacher's lecture. For this reason, students must transcribe the teacher's main points efficiently.

4. Learn what the teacher thinks is important.

   You want to know what the teacher thinks is important because the teacher is the one who will create the test. Most teachers base their tests on their lectures. While some instructors will include a few questions about the textbook, most write tests to correspond to their lectures and handouts.

5. Find out the next class assignments or test questions.

   Many instructors will inadvertently give students information about their test questions during the lecture. If the instructor says that a certain concept is important, students should assume that it will be on the test. In addition, teachers often use their lectures to assign the next week's work or announce quizzes and tests.

6. Forces students to listen carefully.

   Taking good lecture notes requires students to listen carefully to everything the professor says. This helps students to find out what the teacher considers important about the subject and also enables the students to create their own study guides for the tests.

7. Makes students active participants in learning.

   The best students are active participants in their own learning rather than passive sponges that absorb knowledge. Students who actively try to learn the material during the lectures can remember it better for the tests and have an easier time studying for examinations.

8. Better use of time than taping lecture.

Some students do not take notes during class. Instead, they tape the professor's lecture. For most people, this is a waste of time. The student has to sit through the lecture to tape it and then listen to the whole thing again to take notes from it. Taking notes during class is a way to list only the main points of the lecture without all the other pieces that may not be important. Unless students have a learning disability, taping the teacher's lecture is twice as much work as just taking notes.

## The Solutions

An organized method of taking notes can save students a great deal of time and worry. Students who write down everything the teacher says are not working efficiently, while students who write down just a few notes may be missing major concepts.

The following tips will help students take complete notes that will make excellent study guides:

- Be prepared.

  Students who want to take good notes need to have all the appropriate materials with them before class. Be on time and bring plenty of paper and pens. Do the assigned reading or the instructor's lecture will not mean anything.

  In addition, keep all of your notes for one class in one place. If you spread your notes out over several notebooks or keep notes for several classes in the same notebook, you will spend a great deal of your study time just trying to organize your notes.

- Use only one side of a sheet of paper.

  Experts advise that students write on only one side of their paper. You may want to write a summary or include vocabulary words on the back.

- Leave blank spaces between notes.

  The most successful students leave blank spaces in their notes because they will go back and fill in details. After the lecture is over, you may want to summarize the main points, write definitions for the words you did not know or elaborate on concepts that you did not understand. All of this will be much easier if you leave some space in your notes.

- Keep notes brief.

  Do not try to write down everything that the teacher says. Write down just the main points. Sometimes this can be difficult, but err on the side of concision. Do not use whole sentences or even bother with punctuation unless it is important to the subject you are studying.

- Use abbreviations and symbols.
  Feel free to use abbreviations and symbols in your notes to indicate important ideas and keep your notes short. For example, you could use an exclamation point or a star to indicate the major points in the lecture. Write a note to yourself or a key to explain the abbreviations you used so that you can decipher your notes later.
- Note unfamiliar vocabulary words, concepts and other items you do not understand.
  Be sure to include any vocabulary words, main ideas, theories and concepts that the teacher explains. In addition, include anything that you did not understand. Place a question mark next to the item to indicate that you need to ask a question or do more research.
- List all details, definitions and examples.
  If your instructor gives a detailed description of something, a definition or some examples, be sure to write them down. You may be able to use them as support for an essay question on the test. In addition, the details and definitions may not be in the book, so you want to capture them in your notes.
- Write down everything on the board, overhead or PowerPoint® slides.
  If your teacher goes to the trouble of writing information on the chalkboard, on an overhead projector or on PowerPoint slides, be sure to capture all of that information in your notes. Instructors would not bother to do the work unless this particular information was important. If the instructor passes out an outline of the lecture, be sure to fill in the details. You can use the outline as your study guide.

## The Resources

The following resources offer more information about taking notes in class:

*www.csbsju.edu/academicadvising/help/lec-note.htm*

This Website from the College of Saint Benedict and Saint John's University offers useful information about taking notes and identifying the main points of your instructor's lecture.

*www.how-to-study.com/Taking%20Notes%20in%20Class.htm*

This Website offers information about taking notes efficiently during class.

*http://jerz.setonhill.edu/writing/academic/notes-tips.htm*

This Website offers tips on taking notes and includes an excellent bibliography of other sites with further information.

*www.dartmouth.edu/~acskills/success/notes.html*

This Website from Dartmouth College offers a good repository of information about study skills. The section on taking notes is a useful resource.

# Rewriting Your Notes

A junior college student is learning to take good notes in class. However, she finds that her notes do not help her study for the test. Sometimes, she cannot read what she has written, and other times she cannot remember what the abbreviations and marks in her notes are supposed to mean.

She knows that some of her friends rewrite their notes after every class, but she does not think that rewriting her notes will help her remember them better. In fact, she thinks that it would be a waste of time.

This student would like to find a way to make her notes into a useful study guide, but she does not know what to do.

## The Challenge

Keeping up with reading, in-class notes and project work can keep students very busy. Unfortunately, many students do not make time to look at their notes until just before a test. If students do not annotate their notes or rewrite them, they may forget vital pieces of information that may be on the test. In addition, students may forget what their abbreviations and other marks mean.

## The Facts

Experts advise students to review their notes no later than 24 hours after the lecture. In fact, learning professionals suggest that students look at their notes before the next class period in order to add information, explain abbreviations or decipher information in the margins.

Students can increase their retention of the material and the usefulness of their in-class notes greatly if they review their notes. Following are some reasons why this is so beneficial:

Aids in memorization and understanding.

As noted earlier, students can make memorization easier by reviewing the materials frequently. Trying to cram all the information in the few hours or days before the test does not yield good results. The best way to memorize a large amount of material is to do it little by little over a long period.

Can help you answer questions that you noted during the lecture.
Students can make sure that they understand the material by going over their notes and identifying questions that they have. Getting their questions answered as soon as possible will help ensure that they do not fall behind in the class.

Information can be reorganized to suit your preferred learning style.
Whether you are an auditory learner, a visual learner or a kinesthetic learner, you can reorganize and annotate your notes to make them easier for you to study. Visual learners can add color-coding and diagrams. Auditory learners can read them aloud. Kinesthetic learners can rewrite the notes into an outline format.

You can add information that you did not have time to write down in class.
Most professors speak quickly. For this reason, students can easily take notes on the main points but may not have time to write down details or examples from the lecture. However, if students look over their notes right after class or before the next class, they can add information that they did not have time to include in their notes.

You can discover concepts that you do not understand.
Reviewing your notes is an excellent way to find out what you do not understand. Often, students can understand the teacher's notes during the lecture but be unable to explain the key concepts in their own words the next day. If this happens, you will know immediately and can ask the teacher to explain the concept again.

Prepares you for the next class.
In many subjects, the instructor's lecture for one class acts as the foundation for the next class. Each lecture builds upon the information from earlier lectures. Students can help themselves understand all of the concepts better by reviewing the old information before the new information is presented.

You can edit unreadable words or symbols.
Reviewing your notes is a good way to keep them up-to-date. You can change words that you cannot read and add symbols to help you recognize the main points and key terms. If you wait until you are studying for the test, you may not remember what the symbols mean.

You can write out abbreviations.
Using abbreviations in your notes is a good way to keep them brief.

Unfortunately, you may use an abbreviation that you cannot recall later. The best way to make sure that you will be able to understand your notes later is to look them over after class and write out any abbreviations that you think you may forget.

## The Solutions

While some experts advise students to rewrite and reorganize their notes after every class, this method makes the most sense for kinesthetic learners. Researchers suggest that students who are visual or auditory learners only annotate their notes. Following are discussions of both methods.

### Rewriting

Students who learn best by doing should rewrite their lecture notes after every class. These students need to reorganize their notes into an outline format. In this format, each main point should be listed on its own line. Any details or examples for that point should be indented to the right. After skipping a line, the next main point should be listed on its own line. In this fashion, students will be creating their own study guides for the test.

After students have reorganized and rewritten their lecture notes, they need to add references to the appropriate textbook pages, corresponding information from workbooks or handouts and any relevant graphics, images or pictures.

While this method of rewriting lecture notes is geared toward kinesthetic learners, it can work for any student. Interested students should try this method to see if it works for them.

### Annotation

Most students can benefit from annotating their notes instead of rewriting them. This method takes less time but still allows students to customize their notes into study guides for the test.

- Underline.
    First, students need to underline the key points in the notes. This is much easier to do after the lecture is over. During the lecture, students will be trying to write down all the important points and will not be able to underline relevant concepts as well.
- Use symbols to indicate important points.
    Use asterisks, question marks, exclamation points and stars to indicate the main points and concepts in your notes. Arrows and other symbols are also useful in differentiating between several different concepts, theories or examples.
- Color-code your notes.
    Experts advise students to color-code their notes, especially if they are

visual learners. You can organize the colors by subject, date, theory or example.

- Read your notes aloud.
  Students also are advised to read their notes aloud to themselves to help them remember the main points, especially if they are auditory learners. In addition, it can help you recognize places where you have questions or need additional information.

- Coordinate with pages in textbook, handouts or images.
  Make sure to add information about the corresponding textbook pages in each page of lecture notes. Also, add references to handouts from the teacher or graphics in the book.

- Add a key to symbols and abbreviations.
  Add a key in the margin to alert you to symbols, abbreviations and color-coding and what they mean. This will save you stress when you are studying for the test.

- Add summary of the lecture at the end of the notes.
  The very best students add a short summary at the end of each day's lecture notes. This summary can help you study for the test and may prove a useful tool to help you answer essay questions.

## The Resources

The following resources offer more information about rewriting or annotating your notes:

*http://studentaffairs.case.edu/education/resources/onepagers/doc/makingsense.pdf*

This .pdf document from Case Western Reserve University offers information on making sense of your lecture notes. In addition, Case Western offers a host of other one-page study guides on such topics as motivation and time management.

*www.how-to-study.com/Taking%20Notes%20in%20Class.htm*

This Website offers good reasons to rewrite your notes rather than annotating them and includes excellent tips for taking good notes.

*www.ucc.vt.edu/stdysk/editing.html*

This Website explains exactly how to edit lecture notes to make them more useful as study tools.

*www.accd.edu/sac/history/keller/ACCDitg/SSnote.htm*

This Website from Alamo Community College District offers excellent information about rewriting notes and dealing with instructors who talk too fast.

# *16*

# Strategies for Reading Textbooks

A part-time graduate student has more reading than he can do. He frequently skips one reading assignment to catch up on another. Although he knows that he is in danger of falling behind, he does not know how to speed up his reading or organize the way that he takes notes on his textbooks.

The student often finds himself reading the same passage over and over again because he does not remember what he read. This has not helped him to complete his reading assignments any faster.

As final exams draw closer, he is beginning to panic because he cannot keep up.

## The Challenge

Reading multiple textbooks can be a daunting task for even the best students. College texts are complex and long. Students need to be able to read their assignments, take notes and remember what they read in order to be successful. Unfortunately, few students know how to approach a textbook methodically.

One excellent way to read college textbooks was developed in the 1960s. It goes by a variety of names, including SQRW, SQ3R and SQ4R, but the basic premise is the same.

SQRW is an acronym that stands for Survey, Question, Read and Write. Some experts have added another step, as in SQ3R for Survey, Question, Read, Recite and Review. Others have two extra steps, as in SQ4R which stands for Survey, Question, Read, Respond, Record and Review.

## The Facts

The best students understand that the textbook is there to help them learn the material. These students take the time to review each textbook thoroughly even before they begin to read it. Students who look over their books at the beginning of the semester can make the rest of their reading proceed more quickly.

The following tips will help students learn a great deal about their textbooks and make their reading assignments easier:

Read the preface and the introduction.

Does the author mention any special sections, workbooks, CDs or other ancillary materials for the text?

Review the table of contents.

How is the book organized? How many sections does it have, and what do they cover? Does the organizational structure make sense for the subject matter? Does the book list graphics separately? What else can you figure out about the subject from the table of contents?

Check other materials such as a glossary, index or timeline.

Many college texts have additional materials that students may find helpful. For example, does your book have a glossary? Looking up the vocabulary words in the glossary is much easier than having to look them up in a dictionary. Does your book include an index? Choose a topic at random and look it up. Is the index useful? Does the book include a timeline or appendix? Are they useful?

Look for study guides, review questions or additional readings.

Does your textbook include additional readings in the back? What are they? Do they seem interesting or useful? Is there a study guide in the book? What does it cover? Are there review questions? What do they cover? Do they seem useful?

Review chapter headings, sections, summaries and graphics.

Open a chapter at random. Try to choose one that interests you at least a little. Notice how the chapter is organized. College textbook authors work hard to make their books easy to follow because the content is so dense. They often provide four or five levels of headers to divide up the material. All of these divisions help you find the information you need. In addition, they will help you study for the test by organizing the information into logical sections.

Also, look for a summary at the end of each section or chapter. Does your book have one? Is the summary useful? Does your book have learning objectives at the beginning of each chapter? These are excellent roadmaps for studying the chapter. Are the graphics useful? Are they interesting? Are key words or vocabulary bolded in the text? This will help you remember the definitions.

## The Solutions

Once students have looked over their textbooks, they will discover the variety of materials the book provides. Many of these items will prove very useful over the course of the semester.

Going over the textbook before you are assigned any readings will help you speed through the SQ4R method of reading a text. The basic steps are listed below:

Step 1: Survey.

Look over your textbooks. Read the introduction and look at the table of contents. Once you have done this, turn to the chapter you have been assigned and read all of the section headers, look at all of the pictures, read the captions and look over the summary and any review questions. Looking over all the materials will help you to know how the chapter is organized so that you can place the information from the reading in context. Think of this as giving you the big picture of the chapter.

Step 2: Question.

Turn the header of the section you are reading into a question. If the section does not have a header, use the first sentence of the first paragraph. For example, if the header were *Poets of the Romantic Period in England*, your question would be the following: Who were the poets of the Romantic Period in England? Asking a question will help you frame the information you are about to read.

Set 3: Read.

Read the section and look for the answer to your question. This makes you an active learner. If the section is long, you can create a question out of the first sentence in each paragraph or out of subheadings in the text.

Step 4: Respond.

Once you have read the section, close the book and ask your question aloud. Answer it aloud using your own words. This section is called Recite in other versions of SQ3R. You can write down the answer if you prefer. If you cannot answer the question, go back and read the section again. Remember, you are looking for the answer to your question.

Step 5: Record.

When you are certain that you answered your question and understand the material in that section, you can record the information. Some students highlight or underline the text. Other students take notes on what they have read. Still other students write down the summary in their own words.

The advantages of highlighting the text are that it takes less time and allows students to use the graphics to help them study. The disadvantages are that most students either highlight too much of the text or too little and have to go back and re-read sections to study for the test. In addition, students need the textbook itself to study.

The advantages of taking notes on the reading are that the process produces excellent study guides for the test, and students can easily carry them around. The disadvantages are that writing down this information is time-consuming and many students just copy sentences from the text.

Step 6: Review.

A key step in this method is to review your reading notes regularly. In fact, experts advise students to review all of their notes–from the beginning of the semester to the current set of notes–every week. The more often you go over the notes from the first few weeks, the more familiar you will become with this material. In courses that have an all-inclusive final, this type of review is absolutely necessary and will reduce your study time for the final.

## The Resources

The following resources offer more information about how to structure your reading and improve your comprehension:

*www.learningcommons.uoguelph.ca/ByTopic/Learning/Texts/ Fastfacts-SQ4R.html*

This Website from the University of Guelph presents many good study topics for students. Their explanation of the SQ4R reading method is top notch.

*www.dartmouth.edu/~acskills/success/reading.html*

Dartmouth College offers a number of downloadable documents with useful study tips. One of their best efforts is the *Getting to Know Your Textbook* guide at this Website. It also includes a fascinating description of some research that Harvard University did on reading.

*www.ucc.vt.edu/stdysk/sq3r.html*

This Website from Virginia Tech has a good explanation of the SQ3R reading system.

# 17
# Building Your Vocabulary

A college freshman is having trouble with her textbooks. They seem to contain many words that she has never even heard of. She spends so much time looking up words in the dictionary that reading just one chapter takes her 3 hours.

The student thinks that her reading would be completed much more quickly if she knew more of the words. She bought an electronic dictionary, but she is still looking up dozens of words in every assignment. She would like to improve her vocabulary and become a better student, but she does not know where to begin.

## The Challenge

College-level textbooks are dense with definitions, vocabulary terms and information. Reading them takes more time, concentration and motivation than high school textbooks, novels, newspapers or magazines. Students who have small vocabularies will have more difficulty comprehending college texts than those with large vocabularies.

Even the most sophisticated college students will need to look up some words in their textbooks. The difficulty is that looking up words in a print or electronic dictionary takes time. Students with smaller vocabularies can spend up to 50 percent longer reading their assignments.

However, if students work to improve their vocabulary, they can make their study time easier and less complicated. Like studying and memorization requires a method, building a vocabulary can be done with a variety of techniques.

## The Facts

Students with small vocabularies need to build them. A few simple tricks can help them comprehend the meaning of words from their context. Context is how a word is used in a sentence. Many writers also will include a definition of the word within the paragraph.

The best students learn to find clues in the context to figure out what words mean. If the author explains the term within the text, students will not have to look it up. In addition, students can include the new term they have learned in their vocabulary-building exercises. The following seven tips can help students find the meaning of vocabulary words from the text itself:

Definition clue in context.

Some authors will include the definitions of words they think their readers will not understand in the rest of the paragraph. For example, the writer of the next sentence explains that the word *arrears* means behind in their payments:

The landlord told his tenants that they were arrears in their payments because they had not paid the rent in 4 months.

Synonym clue in context.

A synonym is a word that means the same thing as another word. Many authors give a synonym in the paragraph to explain what a difficult word means. For example, in the following sentence, *recalcitrant* means uncooperative:

Sally did not do her homework assignment, but she was recalcitrant or uncooperative when the teacher called on her in class.

Antonym clue in context.

An antonym is a word that means the opposite of a word that the author uses. Some writers include an antonym in their paragraphs to explain vocabulary words by giving their opposites. For example, in the following sentences, the words *sunny skies* help the reader understand that *inclement* means rainy:

George called his friend, Tim, to complain about the inclement weather in Seattle. In return, Tim bragged about the sunny skies in Los Angeles.

Description clue in context.

Sometimes writers include a description to help explain a difficult word in the text. The descriptive words can give you an idea about what the difficult word means. For example, in the following sentences, the description that Tamara never wanted to see her boyfriend again and told her friends that their relationship was over explains that *irrevocable* means final:

Tamara told her boyfriend that their breakup was irrevocable. She never wanted to see him or hear from him again. She told her girlfriends that their relationship was completely over.

Summary clue in context.

Often, authors will include a summary of what a term means by including more information about attributes of the word. For example, in the following sentences, the writer tells enough about the koala that you can tell from the summary that *arboreal* means living in a tree:

Koala bears are arboreal creatures. They eat the leaves of the eucalyptus tree and even sleep in its branches. They do not walk on the ground unless they need to find another tree.

Visual clue in context.

Many authors will include a picture, graph, drawing or chart to explain what a word means. For example, in the following sentence, the writer could give the meaning of the word *arid* by including a picture of a vast desert because arid means without water and plant life:

Most of the country of Saudi Arabia is arid.

Glossary.

In addition to clues in context, students can check their textbooks for glossary pages. Many college textbooks include a glossary with a pronunciation key and definitions for key words in the text.

## The Solutions

Building a better vocabulary is similar to memorizing information for classes. Carry index cards containing your vocabulary words and look at them for a few minutes five or more times a day. Follow the steps below, to improve your vocabulary skills and make your reading easier and more efficient:

Step 1: Be aware of words.

Many people with poor vocabularies do not pay attention to the words around them. The first step to a better vocabulary is to start paying attention to words. Whenever you hear a word that you do not know, write it down on a list, notebook or index card. If you heard someone say it, that word is probably common enough that you need to know it.

Step 2: Read.

Some students think that they can increase their vocabularies just by reading. This is only partly true. Reading can help you find new and interesting words, but it will not necessarily help your vocabulary grow unless you make a serious effort to learn their meanings. Read new magazines, books and newspapers. Identify words that you do not know and write them down.

Step 3: Use dictionaries.

You will need a large collegiate dictionary for home use. You also will need a smaller, paperback dictionary to carry with you. Instead of buying two print versions, you may consider buying an electronic dictionary. If you do this, make sure to buy one that can be expanded. Sooner or later, you will know most of the words, and you will want to add more. Use the dictionaries to look up the meanings of the words you find while reading for pleasure and for school.

Step 4: Use index cards to study.

Write every new word on an index card. Write the word itself on the front of the card. Then write the definition and a sentence using the word on the back of the card. Carry these cards with you wherever you go.

Step 5: Review vocabulary words regularly.

Keep the index cards with you and study them whenever you have a few spare minutes. Look at the word and then try to remember the definition and how it may be used in a sentence. Sort the cards into two stacks. Put the cards containing the words for which you correctly guessed the definitions in one stack and put the cards containing the words that you did not know in the other stack. Keep practicing the words that you do not know until you can remember the definition for every word. If you spend 15 minutes per day reviewing your cards, you will begin to develop a better vocabulary in just a few weeks.

Step 6: Try vocabulary-building books.

Some students have great success with vocabulary-building books or Websites. These can be an excellent help if you find that you enjoy doing the exercises. Before you buy a book, look at the words in it. If you have heard of most of them and have a vague sense of their meaning, buy the book. However, if most of the words are new to you, do not buy the book. You may be frustrated by working with so many words that you do not know and feel discouraged.

Step 7: Use the words.

Two other activities that will help build your vocabulary are using the words in conversation and doing crossword puzzles. According to vocabulary experts, students need to use a word at least 10 times in conversation before the word becomes part of their usable vocabularies. If you have a fairly good vocabulary, you can sharpen your skills by completing crossword puzzles. Start with easier puzzles.

## The Resources

The following resources offer more information about building your vocabulary:

*www.how-to-study.com/Building%20Vocabulary.htm*

This Website is an excellent source for materials about studying, writing papers and memorization. The section on building vocabulary gives good examples of how to understand new words from context.

*http://members.aol.com/jocrf19/steps.html*

This Website from the Johnson O'Connor Research Foundation offers useful tips to help students improve their vocabularies.

# 18

# Factors That Reduce
# Your Reading Rate

A student is having trouble completing the reading for her college classes. Although she always considered herself a good reader, it is taking a long time. She would like to read more quickly, but she is concerned about understanding the material.

The student is thinking about taking a speed-reading class. Information about the class boasts that students can double their reading rate in just 1 month, but it is expensive. She wonders if such an increase is even possible.

## The Challenge

Many college students are concerned about their reading speed. Since they are required to read many chapters per week, college students are often in the market for speed-reading courses. Unfortunately, many students do not need them.

Most students can improve their reading speed by following some simple tips. However, a small percentage of students may read slowly because they have learning disabilities. Students with learning disabilities can be taught how to read more quickly and comprehend more of their reading, but they need to work with learning specialists. Many successful people who have learning disabilities have discovered how to improve their skills with help from experts.

## The Facts

Experts suggest that approximately 6 to 20 percent of American students suffer from some kind of learning disability. These students do not lack intelligence or motivation; their brains simply do not work the same way as most people's do. Because their brains process information in a unique way, these students do not benefit from their classes. However, with advice and training from professionals, these students can be extremely successful.

If you answer yes to several questions in the following list, you may want to consider an assessment from a learning disabilities professional. Many of these professionals work at colleges. Check your school to see what kind of help may be available.

- Do you have trouble following directions?
- Do you have trouble following what your instructor or other people are saying?
- Do you reverse numbers?
- Do you spell words several different ways in the same document?
- Do you have trouble memorizing information and recalling it later?
- Do you have trouble reading newspapers or magazines because the columns are confusing or the print is too small?
- Do you have trouble writing down your ideas and organizing them?
- Do you have trouble copying information because you get similar numbers or letters confused?
- Do you have trouble meeting deadlines or following a schedule?
- Are you impulsive?
- Are you easily distracted and do you have a short attention span?

## The Solutions

Following are some common causes of reduced reading rates and tips that most students can use to improve them:

- Reading environment.

    The physical space where you do your reading can have an enormous impact on your speed. If the light in your space is not adequate, you will fatigue your eyes and only be able to read for short periods of time. The chair you sit in can cause you to fall asleep or become uncomfortable. Either of these problems will cause your reading rate to slow. The temperature in your reading space also can cause you to read more slowly. If you are too warm, you will feel sleepy and read slowly. If you are too cold, your shivering will draw your attention away from your reading and slow your rate.

    In addition, the distance between your book and your eyes also may be a factor. For best viewing, students should hold books at an angle and keep the text at least 18 inches from their eyes. They should wear their glasses if they need them to read.

- Lack of concentration.

    Students read more slowly if they cannot concentrate on the material. Sometimes, this lack of concentration is caused by outside distractions such as students walking by, loud music or conversations.

    Students also can be distracted by emotional stress. Students who are worried about their significant others, parents, money, exams or any other emotional issue may not be able to concentrate, thereby slowing down their reading rates. Learning researchers suggest that students try to put their problems on hold when they are reading. If possible, students are advised to imagine putting their problems in a box and nailing down the cover. When the student is finished reading, he or she can open up the box and deal with the problems.

- Lack of reading practice.
  Students who do not have much practice reading or who read only for school projects may read very slowly. If you do not like to read, then you will not have had much practice. Students need to practice their reading skills in order to improve them.

  Students can improve their speed by reading a wide variety of publications. They can start with easier materials, such as newspapers or magazines, and then progress to novels. Although college textbooks are among the hardest publications to read, students who read a wide variety of materials can improve their reading speed even on difficult texts.

- Vocabulary level.
  Students with a small vocabulary also may read slowly because they do not understand many of the words or have to stop and look them up in the dictionary. Improving your vocabulary will improve your reading speed.

- Comprehension.
  Students with poor reading skills will read more slowly because they will not be able to comprehend the textbook easily. Luckily, most colleges offer classes to help students improve their comprehension. Please note that college reading classes are not about speed-reading. They are about teaching adult students to read and comprehend better.

- Physical state.
  Sometimes a student's physical state is not conducive to reading. For example, students may be tired, sick, recovering from an illness or recuperating from an accident. Students who are dealing with physical pain or illness will not be able to read rapidly because their focus lies outside of the textbook.

- Interest or background knowledge of the material.
  Research has shown that students read information they are interested in much more quickly than information they find dull. In addition, students with little background in the subject area may read more slowly because everything they are reading is new to them.

- Word-by-word reading.

  Students who read word-by-word have a more serious reading problem. Researchers who work with reading skills believe that the fastest readers glance at the written page and read phrases at a time. Students who read word-by-word can improve, but they will need help from reading specialists to change the way they look at text.

- Vocalizing.

  Students who move their lips while reading or whisper the words under their breath also have a more serious reading problem. While reading textbooks aloud can be a useful study tool, always reading this way will keep students reading slowly. Students who vocalize need to work with reading specialists to change their reading habits.

- Regression or re-reading.

  Regression is a serious reading problem, but many students do it. Regression is the process of re-reading words over and over again to get the meaning. Obviously, this process will slow a student's reading rate greatly. Although even good readers do this occasionally, readers who make regression a habit are reducing their reading rate to a crawl. These students can work with reading specialists to increase their reading speed and comprehension.

## The Resources

The following resources offer more information about factors that reduce reading rates:

*http://counseling.binghamton.edu/EFFICIENT%20READING.html*

This Website from Binghamton University offers an excellent selection of reading tips to improve overall reading efficiency, increase speed and explain slower reading rates.

*www.freespeedread.com*

This Website explains clearly why some readers are slower than others.

*www.und.edu/dept/ULC/study/readingrate.html*

This Website from the University of North Dakota, Grand Forks, offers a wealth of information about a wide variety of study skills. Their list of the factors that influence reading rate is a useful summary.

*www.dartmouth.edu/~acskills/success/reading.html*

This Website at Dartmouth College offers a selection of study topics including their handout about how the student's environment affects reading speed.

# 19

# Five R's + 1–
# Record, Reduce, Recite, Reflect, Recapitulate & Review

A bright junior high student has attended every one of her science classes. She tries to listen carefully to everything the teacher says, but she does not think that she is taking good notes.

She jots down the important points and looks at them before the next class, but she would like to be sure that she is doing everything correctly. She would like an organized way to take notes and study from them. She is sure that the other students in her class are taking better notes.

## The Challenge

Every student has trouble taking notes during lectures. Even the best students can write too much or too little. In fact, many students do not pay enough attention to the speaker because they are writing so much.

Any student can learn to take notes in an organized fashion and feel confident that they are getting all of the essential information and that their notes will help them study for and succeed on the tests.

## The Facts

### Three Stages of Listening

Experts believe that students who really listen to a lecture go through three distinct stages: hearing, comprehending and making sense.

*Hearing* involves the physical process of listening to a speaker and hearing the words. For example, if a speaker mentions that koala bears are arboreal creatures, students should remember that information and write it down. If they do this, they are hearing the lecture.

*Comprehending* takes hearing to the next level. In this stage, students try to make sense of what the speaker is saying and determine the important or main points. In this stage, students would want to know what arboreal meant and what other kinds of bears the koala is related to.

*Making sense* is the final step and derives meaning from what has been heard and comprehended. In this stage, the student would look up the definition for arboreal and research the koala bear. The student would discover that arboreal means that koalas live in eucalyptus trees and that they are not bears at all but marsupials.

If students miss any of these steps, they will have difficulty making sense of their lecture notes and studying for tests.

## Taking Notes for Others

Students may find that they pay better attention to lectures and are more successful on examinations when they share their notes. Students who study together or are part of an organized study group may find that they can get even more complete notes if everyone shares.

Students who decide to share notes need to follow even more strict rules about note taking, as others will have to make sense of their writing. The following list includes tips for creating efficient and readable notes to share:

### Format

Format is especially important if you will be sharing your notes with others. You want to make sure that the date, time and subject of the lecture are clearly marked at the top of each page as well as your name. In addition, you need to number your pages and write on only one side. Write neatly and use a dark blue or black ink. This will enable you to copy your notes more easily than if you write in a lighter color.

Draw circles or boxes around the most important ideas or put a star or exclamation point next to them. Leave space between your entries so that you and the other students can add more information or questions later.

### What to Include

Write down anything that the teacher has written down on a chalkboard, overhead or PowerPoint® slide. Write down points that the teacher makes more than once during the lecture. Write down any items that are listed or numbered during the lecture and examples that the instructor gives for each item. In addition, try to get down any vocabulary words and definitions. Even if you think you understand the word, the teacher may be using it in a different context or the word may be used differently in that particular field.

Also, be sure to write down any page numbers in your textbook that the teacher mentions and questions that students ask if you do not know the answer to them. When in doubt or confused about what to write, get down the key verbs and nouns so that you can go back and fill in the gaps later.

### Make a Copy

Never give anyone the only copy of your lecture notes. Make copies for the members of your study group or your study partner, but do not allow anyone else to borrow your notes in order to copy them. How will you study for the test if you never see that student or your notes again?

### Be Sure to Get Copies of Other Students' Notes in Return

If you are sharing notes with a study group or study partner, make sure that you get notes in return. In college, some students identify those who are good in a class and offer to share notes with them. Unfortunately, the students who ask to trade either have no intention of sharing their notes or take such poor notes that no one would want to borrow them. Before you agree to trade and go to the trouble of copying your lecture notes, be sure that you will be getting something worthwhile in return.

## The Solutions

One time-tested method for taking lecture notes is called the Cornell Note Taking System. This technique has been taught, retaught and updated for years because it provides a very useful way to take notes that also allows students to customize the results to use as study guides.

In the Cornell Note Taking System, students take their lecture notes on the 6 inches of space on the right-hand side of the page, which is called the main column. The 2.5 inches of space on the left-hand side of the page is called the recall column. The following steps are used when taking notes:

Step 1: Record.

The first step is to record the lecture in the main column. In this section, students are advised to write down neatly the main ideas, facts and definitions that the teacher mentions in the lecture.

Step 2: Reduce.

Soon after the lecture–ideally immediately after the class–students are advised to summarize the information from the lecture in the recall column. This summary forms the basis of the study material.

Step 3: Recite.

After students have summarized their notes in the recall column, they should cover the main column and recite or say aloud the facts, definitions and main concepts from the lecture in their own words using only the recall column to jog their memories. Then students should uncover the main column and check their answers. This step helps student to remember the most important details of the lecture.

Step 4: Reflect.

After reciting the main points of the lecture, students need to give themselves time to think about what they have learned. Research shows that students who think about their classes and try to categorize or organize what they have learned and tie the information to data that they have learned earlier are well on their way to memorizing the subject for their tests. Our brains work by organizing and categorizing. If students can tie their new knowledge to facts they already know, the new learning will attach to the old and remain in long-term memory.

Step 5: Recapitulate or Summarize.

Some teachers add this as the sixth step to the system. Students write a summary of their lecture notes. They can either summarize each page or write one summary of the whole lecture and include it on the last page of the notes for that day. Students can use the summaries to review for the test.

Step 6: Review.

In this step, students need to do two kinds of review activities. They need to review the information from the most recent lecture immediately and follow the preceding steps. In addition, they need to look over old lecture notes, especially the recall column, so they will not lose the information they learned earlier. Frequent but quick reviews of the old notes will help the student understand the whole course and see how the material is interrelated.

## The Resources

The following resources offer more information about the Cornell Note Taking System:

*www.dartmouth.edu/~acskills/success/notes.html*

This Website from Dartmouth College offers an example of what the Cornell System looks like on a page of notes.

*www.sas.calpoly.edu/asc/ssl/listening.html*

This Website from California Polytechnic University offers excellent insights into the listening and note taking processes.

*www.psych.yorku.ca/upsa*

This Website from the Undergraduate Psychology Students Association at York University includes excellent advice on listening, time management and note taking.

# Common Reading Problems

A worried high school freshman is having reading problems. She cannot seem to organize her work or prioritize her reading assignments. Although she tries to read all of her assignments every night, each one takes hours to complete.

Sometimes she thinks that she may have a learning disability. She was never interested in school until this year and has not been very successful at academics. She thought it was because she did not try hard enough and was more interested in social activities. Now she wonders if she was wrong.

She is thinking about talking to a school counselor and being tested for a learning disability. She does not understand why she works so hard and does not seem to accomplish very much.

## The Challenge

Reading is a difficult process. Although most high school students have been reading for years, many of them are not reading at grade level. Recent studies have shown that students who learned to read under a whole-word reading method do not always read as well as those who learned to read by sounding out words. Teaching strategies for reading have changed in the past several decades because grade school teachers were unhappy with their success rates. Many of them went back to teaching the sounding-out method.

Students who are not good readers or who do not like to read are at a disadvantage in college. Most college classes consist of in-class lectures and reading assignments punctuated with tests or projects. Although some classes require a lab, many classes do not.

Students who do not read well, have a learning disability or exhibit other common reading problems need to consider taking a college reading class. These classes can help students read faster, comprehend better and adapt their reading skills to the type of materials they are reading.

## The Facts

People with learning disabilities account for 6 percent to 20 percent of the general population or approximately 5 to 30 million people. Many of these people have learned to cope with their disability, but this adaptation does not mean that they have learned the skills to read better. In many cases, they have learned to hide their disability.

Students with reading disabilities, especially adults, can be taught to read faster with greater comprehension. First, they need to be tested by a learning disabilities professional. Many of these professionals work at colleges and their services are available to students without charge.

If students find that one or more of the following descriptions apply to them, they should consider being tested for dyslexia, the most common reading problem:

- Does not spell well and looks for others to help correct spelling errors.
- Tries not to write anything out.
- Frequently exhibits excellent verbal language skills.
- May try to hide problems with reading.
- Often exhibits impressive memory skills.
- Frequently shows good skills with other people and exhibits skill at being empathetic or reading people.
- Often has problems with organization, time management and planning.
- Frequently works in a low-level position or at a job below capacity or intelligence.

Many students with reading problems are not native English speakers. These students probably just need more practice or an English as a second language (ESL) class to improve their skills.

## The Solutions

### Common Reading Problems and Learning Disabilities

The most common reading problems are dyslexia, dyscalculia, dysgraphia, dyspraxia and other processing disabilities. Following are descriptions of each:

- Dyslexia
  This is the most common reading problem in the United States. People with dyslexia have trouble reading, spelling, writing, speaking or listening. Sometimes, people who suffer with this disability excel in careers that call for motor skills, visual skills and spatial skills. These students take much longer than their peers to read assignments in college textbooks.

- Dyscalculia
  People with this common learning disability have trouble doing simple arithmetic and understanding basic math concepts. This disability makes

it difficult to do everyday things such as balancing a checkbook or figuring out how much money to get from the ATM. These students may have difficulty with time management as well. They may not allow enough time to read the assignment or may read the wrong chapters.

- Dysgraphia
  People with this common learning disability have trouble forming letters or writing in a confined space such as an employment application. If given more time to complete written work, these students can write neatly. These students have difficulty taking notes when they read, which can lead to problems studying for the examination.

- Dyspraxia
  This learning disability involves the person's motor skills. This may make it difficult for the student to hold a book or sit for a long period and read.

- Auditory, memory and processing disabilities
  People with these types of learning disabilities often have trouble understanding words they read or remembering words once they have read them. This disability can be misperceived as a hearing problem.

## Categories of Learning Disabilities

In general, all of these common reading problems fall into one of three categories: decoding, comprehension and retention. Decoding problems involve the inability of students to understand what the letters mean, how the letters form words and how to decipher what the words mean. Common decoding problems include:

- Difficulty sounding out words and recognizing words out of context;
- confusion between letters and the sounds they represent;
- slow oral reading–reading word-by-word;
- reading without expression; and
- ignoring punctuation in text.

Comprehension problems are directly related to decoding problems. Students who have difficulty decoding can find it almost impossible to understand what they have read or remembering it as well. Common comprehension problems include:

- Confusion about the meaning of words;
- difficulty connecting ideas in a paragraph or selection;
- leaving out or glossing over details;
- trouble determining which details are important and which are not; and
- inability to concentrate when reading.

Retention problems are frequently a result of comprehension and decoding problems. Students who cannot recognize words, phrases or sentences also will have problems understanding those items in a reading selection. As students go through school, they are required to read, remember and comment on more and more material. Students who cannot keep up with the increasing assignments often fall behind. Common retention problems include the following:

- Trouble remembering or summarizing reading;
- trouble attaching present reading with something learned earlier; and
- trouble applying content of reading to day-to-day life.

## Impact of Common Reading Problems

Students with these common reading problems or learning disabilities can find that the following areas of their lives are affected by their disability:

- Personal

  Students with learning disabilities often have low self-esteem. They frequently strive to keep out of situations in which they may be embarrassed again by their disability.

- Education

  These students may not have been successful in academic situations. They may have found that teachers did not expect much of them or expected too much.

- Career

  People with low self-esteem do not like to take chances. They may stay in a low-level job because they do it well or do not want to look for another position.

- Social/Interpersonal

  Many people with learning disabilities also have problems with interpersonal relationships. For example, they may not understand or be able to tell jokes. Their interactions with other people are frequently so difficult that they cannot establish ongoing relationships.

- Everyday living

  Some people with learning disabilities have little difficulty operating in the adult world. However, some may have trouble filling out tax forms, writing checks, balancing a checkbook and managing other everyday chores.

## The Resources

The following resources offer more information about specific reading problems and learning disabilities:

*www.philseflsupport.com/reading_approaches.htm*

  This Website is for ESL students and teachers, but it offers an excellent selection of materials about common reading problems.

*www.interdys.org/servlet/compose?section_id=5&page_id=44*

  This Website from the International Dyslexia Association offers a wide variety of tools and resources for those who suffer from dyslexia and their families.

*21*

# Improving Your Reading Skills

A fifth-grader has been tested, and she does not have a learning disability. The professional who tested her suggested that she take a reading class.

She is thinking about taking the course, but she is embarrassed and feels as if she has been held back a grade. She does not want to look foolish and worries that her friends will find out. While she would like to read better and more quickly, the student is afraid that others, including the teacher, will make fun of her.

## The Challenge

Most students can improve their reading skills by following just a few simple tips. Even students with learning disabilities can improve their reading rate and comprehension with help from a specialist.

In fact, all college students could benefit from a reading course. They would lean how to take efficient notes during a lecture and also how to take notes while reading a college textbook. Reading classes also offer advice about reading more quickly while gaining even better comprehension of the material.

Because college students have been reading for so long, many of them have fallen into bad habits, such as holding their books too close, not wearing their prescription lenses when reading or rereading the same sentences over and over again. With practice and advice from a reading specialist, students can increase their speed, comprehension and note taking ability.

## The Facts

Many students believe a variety of myths about the reading process and refuse to change their habits despite a great deal of research to disprove each of myths.

The following are the six most common myths about reading:

> Myth 1: Students must read every word of the chapter.
> This is patently untrue. Many words in college textbooks are unnecessary. For this reason, most structured reading methods ask students to skim

or scan the chapter first to get the general idea of the topic or answer specific questions. However, this does not mean that they only should answer review questions and ignore the rest of the text. Some college textbooks repeat the main ideas over and over again. Students can save a great deal of time if they can scan the text and identify them.

Myth 2: Students only need to read chapters once.
This is also untrue. However, students should not read every chapter twice either. Be selective in your reading. Read a section at a time and quiz yourself. If you have scanned the material in the beginning, you will have an overview of the topic and can then plug the pieces you read into your overall understanding. If you relate the information to facts that you have already learned or concepts that you understand, the material will move from your short-term memory into your long-term memory.

Myth 3: Students cannot skip sections.
The purpose of reading your textbook is to get the main ideas out of it. If you can get the main ideas from the headings and graphics, you do not need to read the rest of the chapter. Some successful students only read all the headings, the captions on the pictures and graphics, and the first sentence of every paragraph. They often can find the main ideas of the assignment just by taking these steps. In many textbooks, the first sentence of a paragraph, or topic sentence, explains what the whole paragraph is about. The rest of the paragraph will elaborate on the topic sentence or give examples and details. If your textbook is written like this, you can sift through the main ideas quickly.

Unfortunately, many students feel guilty if they do not read every word of the assignment. College is a time to learn to work smart, not just hard. Not all textbooks will make your job easy. If you find such a book, feel free to skip sections.

Myth 4: Students need speed-reading classes to be efficient readers in college.
This is not true. Students who want to increase their reading speed need to push themselves to read faster. They can do this by using an index card to help their eyes move more quickly across the page. Some students use their finger or a bookmark for the same purpose. Make sure that the index card is moving to speed up your eyes and that your eyes are not causing the index card to move along with them.

Myth 5: Students who read quickly or skim cannot comprehend the material.
There is little correlation between reading speed and comprehension. Some students read quickly and comprehend well. Other students read slowly and do not comprehend the material at all. Skimming or scanning the text is an excellent way to find the main ideas and the details that support them and help you read more quickly.

Myth 6: Students' eye problems cause them to have a lower reading rate.
Eye problems are seldom the cause of slow reading rates. The cause most often is that the student reads word-by-word or reads the words aloud. As noted earlier, reading aloud is an excellent technique for auditory learners, but it will take a great deal of time to read every assignment this way.

Students who wear their prescription lenses can read quickly if they try. In general, it is the brain that controls the reading rate and not the eyes. Research has shown that the brain is able to read much faster than most students are used to reading. Students usually need practice scanning and skimming to increase their reading speed.

## The Solutions

Students who want to read more quickly and improve their comprehension can do so with a little advice from reading experts. Students can improve their overall reading rate by following the tips below:

Vary your reading rate.
Good readers do not read everything at the same rate. They read at different speeds for different purposes. For example, skimming and scanning can be done at a high rate of speed. Reading quickly is also appropriate for finding a specific piece of information.

Students may read quickly through material that is familiar to them. For example, you may know a great deal about sub-Saharan deserts because you did a science project on them in high school. If you have to read a whole chapter on the subject, you will be able to move quickly because you are already familiar.

Slow down when reading information that is new or complex. You may need to figure out complicated sentence structures, technical descriptions or abstract theories. However, you probably do not need to read every example or detail slowly. One or two are usually enough to give you the general idea. Unless you are reading a section in order to remember specific information for a test, you do not need to read all of the material slowly.

If you run into a word that you do not understand, you may be able to discover the meaning from its context within the paragraph. Many authors include information to explain terms that their readers may not understand. Also, be alert for glossaries in the back of the book.

Follow an organized reading method.
The best way to improve your reading is to follow an organized reading method such as the Cornell System. These organized methods advise

students to scan title headings and first sentences to get the big picture of what the chapter is about. Students are then asked to form questions and answer those questions while reading.

Research indicates that students who can organize or categorize new information from the beginning find it easier to store it in long-term memory. Learning experts know that the brain organizes ideas and details by category or type. If students learn material in this fashion, they will remember more of it with less effort.

Do not highlight everything.

Many students make the mistake of underlining or highlighting too much of their textbook. If the entire page is highlighted, students will find it difficult to study the main ideas for a test. You can improve your reading if you highlight or underline only the main ideas, one or two examples that explain each one and vocabulary words that you do not already know.

Jot down information in the margins.

Use the margins in your textbook to write down questions you have or summaries of the material. You also can use this space to put the main ideas into your own words. Some students write all of this information in their notes. Practice either method with every reading assignment.

Coordinate chapter reading with workbooks, labs, ancillary materials and in-class lecture notes.

The best way to improve your reading is to make sure that all the information you have is correlated. For example, your textbook should reference the relevant sections of your lecture notes and vice versa. This will increase your reading rate because you will have to look up information only once and then write it down. In addition, this method will greatly enhance the value of your notes and the textbook as study materials for tests.

## The Resources

The following resources offer more information about how to improve reading rate and comprehension:

*www.psywww.com/mtsite/rdstratg.html*

This Website from Mind Tools offers a great deal of information about increasing the speed of your reading and learning how to adjust your speed to the material.

*www.muskingum.edu/~cal/database/general/reading.html*

This Website from Muskingum College offers a large amount of information about learning strategies and reading comprehension.

# 22

# Remembering What You Read

A high school honors student is having trouble remembering the poems in her English class. She is supposed to be able to remember at least 50 poems this semester. She does not need to recite all the poems from memory, but she must be able to recognize a line or two from each poem and write down its title or the name of the poet.

While she has read and reread the poems and the biographical information about each poet a number of times, she is having trouble keeping all the information straight in her head. She wishes that she could find a way to remember what she reads without having to reread the material over and over again.

## The Challenge

Students are required to read more and more as they progress in school. High school classes require students to read textbooks and literature. College classes require students to read textbooks, literature, academic journal articles and scientific articles. With all of these different types of reading, students need to be able to remember a great deal of what they read.

All students can remember more of what they read if they follow the steps listed below. Many of these techniques have been discussed in other sections of this book.

## The Facts

Students retain more of their reading assignments when they cultivate the following four reading skills:

1. Purpose.
   Before you pick up a textbook, you need to know why you are reading it. The obvious answer is because the teacher and the course outline require it. However, you also need to come up with a purpose for yourself. Think about what you want to get out of the text.

As much as possible, try to work smart not work hard at reading. Many textbooks will provide outlines, learning objectives, summaries and review questions. Use these tools to learn the key points without having to read every single word of each chapter.

2. Motivation.

Students who complain that they cannot remember what they read sometimes are not motivated. Your personal reasons for succeeding as a student depend largely on your attitude. If you approach your reading with a good attitude, you will be more successful. In turn, you will feel more confident that you can find the main ideas in the textbook, and this confidence will fuel future successes. If you tell yourself that you can remember what you read and you expect this result, you will be successful. However, if you expect to forget everything quickly, you will set yourself up for failure. Stay motivated and you will retain more.

3. Concentration.

Even some good students say that they cannot concentrate when they read. The problem is not concentration. Experts have proved that all students can concentrate when they are reading an article in a magazine they like. The difficulty is concentrating when the subject matter is complex, dull or not to the student's taste.

A good attitude, appropriate motivation and the will to succeed can help you concentrate on any textbook in any subject. More complex texts may require you to read more slowly or stop after each small section to rethink what you have read, but you can read anything you want to. Minimizing distractions will help. Turn off electronic gadgets, computers and telephones. Ignore other people and put your emotions on hold.

4. Sorting and categorizing.

Research has shown that the brain organizes new learning into categories. Students can attach their new learning to old information they were taught before. Students who want to remember what they read need to do their own sorting and categorizing.

As you read a textbook, think about how this new information fits in with what you have learned in other chapters or in other courses. Try to categorize what you are reading into sections or groups. For example, poetry could be classified by the subject of each poem—love, the beauty of nature, etc. You could then construct a mnemonic device to help you remember the poems and the names of the poets for each subject area

Categorizing the poems as you read them, will tell your brain where to store the information. In fact, you will help your brain skip the sorting step because you have already done so. Now, your brain can concentrate solely on remembering the poems. If you are an auditory learner, you also may consider reading the poems aloud.

## The Solutions

Students who want to remember what they read need to ignore many of the myths about reading textbooks. One of these myths is that students need to read every word of every chapter, and another is that students must begin reading on the first page of their assignment.

The following steps will help students organize their reading so that they will be able to remember what they read more easily and completely:

Step 1: Get an outline of the chapter first.

Look over your chapter without beginning the reading. If possible, read the summary section or the review questions first. These pieces will tell you what the main ideas are. Some students look through the chapter to answer the review questions before they begin to read the chapter.

This process works best if you think of the chapter outline as a skeleton. You are looking over the skeleton of the chapter first and then bit-by-bit you will fill in the various organs and the skin.

Step 2: Visualize as you read.

No matter what you are reading, visualize it as you read. For example, imagine the various battles in a history class. Think of the images being presented in literature or poetry. Form a picture in your mind of the scientific experiments you may be reading about. Whatever the subject, you can remember the text better if you visualize the actions in your mind.

If you prefer, think of it as making a movie or a music video in your head. Washington can be crossing the Delaware River with a guitar in his hand. Keats can be describing a Grecian urn with a microphone hanging over his head. Funny images will stick in your memory longer.

Step 3: Practice recitation.

Recitation is not reading aloud. Recitation is stopping every so often in your reading, usually at the end of a section, and summarizing what you have read in your own words. Some students cover the book during this exercise and then check their answers. Other students write down their summary in order to use it for a study guide.

However you decide to organize it, you need to put the material in your own words for two reasons. First, you will be able to remember your own words better. Second, if you can summarize what you have learned, then you have really learned it.

The best and most effective summaries are done aloud, so choose a quiet place where you will not disturb others. Even students who are not auditory learners can benefit from this recitation technique.

Step 4: Schedule repetition.

Practice, practice, practice. You do not want to memorize your recitation, but you want to go over the information from the reading again and again. Use notecards or flashcards. Write a summary of each section or the whole chapter. Take notes on the main points in each section after you have done your recitation. Choose the method that works best for you and practice with every single chapter that you have to read.

## The Resources

The following resources offer more information about remembering what you read:

*www.csbsju.edu/academicadvising/help/remread.htm*

This Website from the Academic Advising Center at the College of Saint Benedict and Saint John's University gives useful advice about remembering what you read and concentrating on your reading.

*www.canberra.edu.au/studyskills/learning/reading*

This Website from the University of Canberra, Australia offers insight into the reading process and how to move information from short-term to long-term memory.

*www.how-to-study.com/flexiblereading.htm*

This Website explains the various sorts of reading that a typical student might do for college classes.

*http://academic.cuesta.edu/acasupp/AS/311.HTM*

This Website from Cuesta College in California explains how to remember what you read more efficiently and effectively.

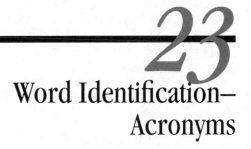

# Word Identification– Acronyms

A premed student is trying to study for a difficult science exam. She has attended every class and taken good notes. She has reviewed her notes after every class or before the next one. She also has read every textbook chapter.

Even though she has done everything correctly, she is worried that she will forget one or more of the complicated formulas and lists that she needs to know for the test. She has joined a study group, but everyone in it is half her age. The group has helped her, but she thinks that the younger students are smarter than she is.

This student needs to find a way to remember long and complicated information so that she will feel confident during her exam.

## The Challenge

Good students can succeed in most classes by using the skills of repetition and review, taking good notes and reading their textbooks. However, complicated topics with a great deal of information that needs to be remembered can be difficult for even the most gifted students.

Learning experts have created a number of memory tricks to help students remember more complex information. These devices are called mnemonics. Several of these mnemonics have been discussed in other chapters.

By using one or more of these memory tricks, students can remember long lists of information. Try out each method and see which ones work for you. Your preferred learning style also will help you determine which methods will be most helpful.

## The Facts

### Imagery and Visualization

One trick to improve the effectiveness of mnemonics is to add images to them. This technique is called imagery or visualization. Although this method will work better for visual learners, it also can be effective for students who are auditory or kinesthetic learners.

The following list includes tips for improving memory through imagery:

Tip 1: Use funny images.
> Use the silliest image you can think of to help you remember information. Funny images stick in your brain. If you can tie the information that you have to memorize to a funny visual image, you will remember the image and the information it represents more easily. Besides, the silly image will make you smile during the test, and smiling will help you relax.

Tip 2: Use strange, weird and colorful images.
> Strange or weird images are more vivid, and vivid images are easier to remember. If you can picture the image and feel as if you are really seeing it, you can recall large chunks of information associated with it.

Tip 3: Create different environments for different classes.
> One concern for students is remembering information for the wrong class. You can make sure that you do not confuse the images from one class with another by using different environments for each one. For example, use a circus for one class and a water amusement park for another. Tie the imaginary environment to the subject itself as much as possible. You might use a spaceship for an astronomy class, a zoo for a zoology class, Victorian England for an English literature class, etc.

Tip 4: Use as many senses as possible.
> Try to add all your senses to the image. Sound, smell, taste, touch, emotions and three-dimensional images make mnemonics more vivid and easier to remember. Add emotions as well. Are some of your imaginary characters angry or upset about their fictional situation? Adding someone with bad cologne, an off-key singing voice or a strong emotion to express will help you to remember the image and the information more easily.

Tip 5: Make images larger than life.
> Create larger-than-life images to help you remember them. Include giants, elves, dwarves—anything or anyone that you will find amusing.

Tip 6: Add a silly song or jingle.
> Images come to life if you add a silly song or a jingle. It can contain the information that you need to memorize. Before written language, singers were the historians. They created songs with rhyme and melody to record significant historical events.

## The Solutions

Mnemonics help students remember information and save it in their long-term memories. Following are some of the most common mnemonic tricks:

### Acronyms

Acronyms in mnemonics mean the same as they do elsewhere. You can create acronyms when you try to memorize information for classes. Many students learned the colors of the rainbow in the correct order by remembering the name *Roy G. Biv*, which stands for red, orange, yellow, green, blue, indigo and violet. Use the first letters of a phrase or list to create a name that stands for the information you need to remember.

### Acrostics

Acrostics are acronyms that go together in a sentence. For example, many students have learned the names of the notes of the treble clef staff using the acrostic *Every Good Boy Deserves Favor*, which stands for the notes on the lines: E, G, B, D and F.

### Rhyme or song

Human beings respond to rhythm, rhyme and songs. You can use this to your advantage, especially if you are an auditory learner, by creating a rap song, a silly jingle or a song that includes all the information that you have to learn.

Your song will be even more memorable if you imagine a music video to help you remember the song and the information. For example, students used to learn this spelling rule in rhyme: I before E except after C or when sounded as in neighbor and weigh.

You do not have to dream up the melody yourself. Use a common tune or a song that you learned in childhood. The melody is not important. It is just the vehicle to help you remember the data.

### Method of Loci

This memorization technique is almost as old as recorded history. The great Roman and Greek speakers used this method to help them remember long speeches. Choose a path that you are very familiar with. Visualize each landmark along your path. Where are the most beautiful flowers? Where is the biggest automobile? What are the names of the streets? Where is the nearest gas station or drug store?

As you visualize each location, assign a piece of information to it. Imagine the information that you need to remember being in this specific location. Do this with each piece of information or list that you have to memorize.

If you practice this technique, you will be able to assign longer and longer lists to each site. The key is that you have to know the path intimately.

### Chunking

Learning experts believe that people can remember seven items plus or minus two in their short-term memories. So, people can remember from five to nine items at once. However, if you chunk a great deal of information into each of those seven items, you can make yourself remember more information in the same space.

This method works well for number-related information, but it can work for any other type of list. The idea is to increase the size of each of the seven items into a long string. You can think of a long string of numbers as the score to a game, as a year that something happened or as a telephone number. You also can use acronyms or acrostics to help you remember a string of words for each of the five to nine items.

### Repetition

This method of memorization is even older than the Method of Loci. Repeating information over and over again aloud is a good way to remember it. However, if you have a great deal of information to remember, you can improve your retention rate by adding imagery, rhythm or a song to the repetition.

### Flashcards

Flashcards are a powerful memory tool. Write questions on one side of the cards and the answers on the other side. Take the cards with you, and go over them quickly whenever you have a few minutes. In a short time, you will be able to memorize the information on the cards.

This method will help you learn a large amount of information, but it takes time and does not work well if you are experiencing the stress of a test in the next day or two.

## The Resources

The following resources offer more information about mnemonic devices and other learning tools:

*www.utexas.edu/student/utlc/class/mkg_grd/mnemonic.html*

This Website from the University of Texas offers a huge list of learning techniques.

*www.thememorypage.net/acro.htm*

This Website offers a long list of useful acronyms.

*www.ncsu.edu/studenthandbook/success/topics_memory.php#acronyms*

This Website from North Carolina State University offers a variety of study materials including this section on acronyms and other memory tools. It is also a useful resource for managing your time during the stress of college.

# 24

# Studying in a Group

A young man is having difficulty passing his math class. Although he studies every day, he seems to forget everything when he looks at the test. He can do the sample problems without difficulty, but he seems to freeze up when he sees similar problems on the exam.

He also finds that he cannot accurately predict what will be on the test. He practices the particular kind of problem he expects to see on the test, but that type of problem either is not included or represents only a few points.

He has heard that there is a study group for his class, but he is concerned that he will appear stupid to the other students. He thinks that it is probably more of a social club than a study group.

## The Challenge

Study groups are almost always an excellent way for students to help each other succeed. They can provide a way for students to teach each other the material and learn it themselves. They also allow students to share the study load and motivate one another to succeed. Study groups also provide opportunities for students to practice active listening skills and cooperation.

## The Facts

To ensure that your study group is useful to you and your fellow students, follow a method similar to the one below, whether you create your own group or join an existing one:

Keep your group small.
> Studies have shown that study groups of three to six people work best for most classes. Two people are too few because the group cannot function if one person is absent. Eight people are too many. Everyone in your study group should be signed up for the same class.

Choose a leader to run the group.

Research suggests that groups work best when one person is in charge of keeping everyone on track. Some groups succeed by having the leadership role handled by different members at each meeting. The trouble with this method is that people could get confused about who is supposed to lead the group, or the leader for a particular session could be unable to attend.

Create an agenda for each meeting.

Preparing an agenda may seem too formal for a typical study group, but the agenda is merely a schedule for the meeting. Just as students need to create schedules to accomplish their goals, your study group needs to create a schedule to meet its goals. The agenda should include the meeting date, the time and an outline of what group members are responsible for presenting along with any other items that the group will discuss during the meeting.

Some study groups go over old homework assignments, drill each other on key concepts and ask one another open-ended questions about the material. Study groups also may create quizzes to help the group study for a test or the final exam. Whatever you decide to accomplish, an agenda will help keep the group on track.

Allow students to give presentations.

Many study groups work by asking each student to present material from the textbook or the classroom lectures. The advantage of this is that the student doing the presenting must learn the material thoroughly in order to present it. In addition, the student presenter may explain the concepts in a different way than the instructor does, and this diversity will help all the students learn better. Some of the students in the group may not have understood what the professor was trying to say, but these students may be able to comprehend the concepts when they are presented in different words by a fellow student.

Keep the meetings to 1 or 2 hours.

Just as students should take breaks while studying, study groups should not meet for long periods of time. Meeting for too long will hurt individual motivation and may undermine what the group is trying to do. Meeting once a week or several times a week for just 1 or 2 hours is adequate for students to be able to help one another.

Plan the next meeting before everyone leaves.

The last item on the agenda for each meeting should be to plan the next meeting. The leader should assign work, choose a date and time, and make sure that everyone can attend.

## The Solutions

Although the advantages far outweigh the disadvantages, study groups need to be run efficiently to be successful. If students spend too much time discussing the professor or other topics unrelated to their studies, the group can waste a great deal of time.

To help you and your group be successful, make sure that everyone in your study group agrees to the following rules:

Rule 1: Do not interrupt one another.
> To be successful, your study group needs to be respectful of every member. For this reason, many groups do not allow anyone to interrupt when another member is speaking. Questions are allowed at the end of a presentation.

Rule 2: Avoid hangers-on.
> Many students equate group study with group projects they may have done in high school. Often, one or two students in the group did all the work on these projects while others barely participated. Study groups are no place for people who do not want to work. Make sure that everyone in the group understands what the group will do and what is expected of every member.

Rule 3: Create a diverse group.
> The best groups are made up of people with diverse backgrounds. The more diversity your group has, the more opportunities there will be for the group to learn. People who are older or culturally different may have interesting and worthwhile insight into the classroom material. In addition, workplaces are diverse. The more you are able to cooperate with people of different backgrounds and ethnicities, the better an employee and manager you will be in the future.

Rule 4: Everyone must read all the assignments.
> Some study groups divide the reading assignments among the members. Each member only reads one section and presents the materials to the other members. However, if the person who is supposed to present a section is unable to attend, the whole group will be missing a portion of the material. Also, if the student presenter leaves out any major points, the entire group will suffer.

> Research clearly shows that study groups work best when the whole group reads all the assignments and attends all the lectures. Group members can ask questions of the student presenters and fill in any gaps in their understanding before the test.

Rule 5: Do not make critical or personal comments about others.
Working with other students can be stressful, especially at the end of the term. Rude remarks or personal attacks will weaken your group and hurt your ability to work together. Do not allow them. The world is made up of a huge variety of people. To get along with all these people, you need to be respectful of other people's learning styles, communication methods and abilities.

Rule 6: Do not complain about the class, the assignment or the examinations.
One mistake that some study groups make is allowing members to complain about the class. No matter how difficult the subject or the professor, no one makes it easier by complaining. The group can make progress and help everyone succeed by working together within the constraints of the material and the class.

Rule 7: No socializing until the meeting is over.
Another major mistake that some study groups make is allowing members to socialize before the work is completed. With luck, you will enjoy your study group and like the people who are in it. However, if you spend time socializing, you will be unable to help one another succeed in class. For this reason, it is best to choose a strong group leader who does not allow any chitchat until the work is done. Study first, and play later.

## The Resources

The following resources offer more information about the specifics of setting up or joining a study group:

*www.math.yorku.ca/new/undergrad/studygroups.htm*

This Website from York University in Toronto offers insight into the importance of working with a group and how the group can improve individual student performance.

*www.tcd.ie/Student_Counselling/docs/study_groups.pdf*

This Website from Trinity College in Dublin explains group study in great detail. They even offer a list of guidelines for setting up your own study group.

*www.coun.uvic.ca/learn/program/hndouts/studygr.html*

This handout from the University of Victoria in British Columbia explains how a study group can increase your learning. In addition, this Website offers practical advice about how to keep groups from falling into bad habits.

# 25

# Getting Additional
# Help from Your Teacher

A college student is having trouble with his philosophy class. He does not understand the reading assignments, even though he reads them several times. He understands most of what the instructor says in class, but the information seems to evaporate when he leaves the classroom.

Although he thinks the professor is odd because of the way he dresses, the student is thinking about asking him for help. He is concerned that the teacher may be even more bizarre in person than he is in class.

## The Challenge

Student-teacher relationships are a two-way street. The teacher's part of the relationship is to teach, help students and grade their performance. The student's part is to do his or her best to learn the material and be an active learner.

Creating a good impression for the teacher is just as important in college as it is in high school, especially if the class is small. If your class is in a large lecture hall, create a good relationship with your professor's teaching assistant. The TA is your first stop when you need help.

## The Facts

While you do not know whether or not you will need help at the beginning of the semester, creating a good relationship with your teacher early on will better enable you to ask for help later. Following are some tips to help you establish good relationships with your instructors so that you can go to them for help at any time:

Teachers are people too.

This may seem obvious, but teachers are people too. The truth is that few students ever come to talk to their professors outside of class. Your teacher will be interested in talking to you, and you will stand out because you took the time to create a personal relationship with them.

Some experts have referred to the student-teacher relationship as a business relationship. It is all about the business of the course you are taking. You both are in the relationship to get something out of it.

The student wants to learn the material. The teacher wants to teach the material. The common ground is helping the other person achieve his or her goal.

Go to office hours once or twice during the semester.

Before you need help, visit the instructor during office hours. College teachers usually list their office hours on the course syllabus, or their office doors, so that students will know when they are available.

Ask the instructor about the subject, research interests, personal interests or teaching background.

While you are there, talk about the course requirements and the subject. Try to find something out about the teacher as a person. What are his or her research interests? Why did this person go into teaching?

Getting to know your instructors as people is a good way to practice skills that you will use later in life. You will work with many different kinds of people. Learning how to talk with and learn from people who are different than you is an excellent skill to cultivate. Besides, many teachers are interesting people in their own right.

Do not visit right after class or just before examinations.

Some teachers tell their students to ask questions right after class. Others want to be visited during office hours. Be polite. Ask the teacher after class if you can make an appointment. If the teacher has time, he or she may answer questions right away. Remember that teachers also have many administrative responsibilities. Your instructor may be running to teach another class or going to a departmental meeting.

Try not to visit the professor for the first time just before a test, project or examination. Teachers get annoyed if students do not ask questions or seem interested in the class until just before a big test. Visit the professor at the beginning of the semester. If you have questions or concerns later in the term, you can visit the professor during office hours. Your first visit tells the teacher that you are genuinely interested in being a good student and creating a good relationship.

Show teacher that you are interested in the subject.

Visiting your teacher early in the semester shows that you want to create a good working relationship. Now, you need to show him or her that you are a good student. You can do this by trying your hardest to learn the materials doing all of the following:

- be on time
- turn in assignments on time
- ask good questions in class
- pay attention to the teacher during lectures
- do the homework
- do the assigned reading
- take notes

In most cases, teachers want to help their students succeed. However, some teachers, especially those teaching college classes, will not make an effort unless the student has done his or her part. Even gifted instructors cannot teach students who are not making an effort.

## The Solutions

Students who create a good impression at the beginning of the term are in a much better position to ask for help later in the semester. Follow the steps below to get help from instructors and to prepare yourself so that you get the most out of any help session:

### How to Get Help from Teachers

Make sure you did your part.

> Before you ask a teacher for help, make sure that you did everything you could to learn the material. Did you do all the reading? Did you attend all the lectures? Did you do all the homework? Did you study the material? If you answered yes to every question, you have tried to learn the material.

Go to the TA first.

> If your class has a teaching assistant, you should go to this person first for help. In most instances, the TA will be a graduate student who is majoring in the subject of your course. TAs also have office hours posted on their doors. If you have a lab class with the TA, be sure to ask if you can set an appointment. If you just go during his or her office hours, you may have to wait for other students.

Go during office hours and ask for help.

> If your class is not large enough for a TA, go to your teacher's office hours or make an appointment. Making an appointment will ensure that you have a specific time to talk with the teacher one on one.

### Be Prepared for Your Help Session

Once you have made your appointment or arrived at the teacher's office, make sure that you are prepared to explain exactly what is confusing you. Follow the steps below to organize your thoughts:

Step 1: Do not waste their time.

> Professors and TAs are busy. They have courses to teach, papers to grade and administrative responsibilities to deal with. When you go to visit them during office hours, be prepared to get right to the point about what you do not understand.

Step 2: List your questions.

> Prepare a list of questions. Unlike high school, you do not want to visit a professor and simply say that you do not get it. Teachers at this level expect you to be responsible for your own learning.

Step 3: Identify the specifics of what you do not understand.

Be specific about what you do not understand. Bring your book and mark passages that confuse you. If this is a math class, bring problems that you have completed and include all of your calculations. If this is a writing class, bring the paper you are working on. Try to figure out exactly what you do not understand so that the teacher can try to explain it to you in a different way or with different words.

Step 4: Listen carefully and ask questions to clarify.

Listen carefully to the professor's explanations. Ask questions to ensure that you understand the information.

Step 5: Summarize what the teacher is saying.

Ensure that you understand new material by summarizing the information and saying it back to the teacher. If the teacher corrects your summary, be sure to ask more questions to clarify your understanding of the material.

Step 6: Thank the teacher.

Thank the teacher or TA for their help and be sincere. In college, the professor does not have to provide extra help. Most professors do this because they are dedicated to teaching.

Step 7: Ask if you can come back if you have more questions.

Before you leave, ask if you can return again if you have more questions. If you have prepared yourself and been specific, the teacher will want to help you again. Most teachers do not mind having students come by to ask questions from time to time. However, students who visit frequently to ask the same or similar questions can be annoying. No matter what level you are at in school, it is unwise to annoy the person who will be grading you.

## The Resources

The following resources offer more information about asking teachers for help:

*http://people.westminstercollege.edu/faculty/pconwell/teaching/Maximizing% 20Your%20Undergraduate%20Academic%20Experience.htm*

This excellent Website from Westminster College offers good advice for all undergraduate students about getting along with professors and TAs.

*http://kidshealth.org/kid/feeling/school/getting_along_teachers.html*

Although this information is written for grade school students, the material is applicable to high school and college students. This Website explains in detail how to get along with your teachers.

# 26

# Getting Additional Help from a Tutor

A college sophomore is having more trouble with her science class. She has spoken to the teacher and the teaching assistant, but they seem to explain everything at too high a level. The student barely understands what they are saying.

Her parents think it is time for her to get a tutor, but she does not know how to go about finding one. She also is concerned that the tutor will not be able to explain the material any better than her teacher or TA can.

## The Challenge

Students who are having trouble with a class need to ask for help as soon as possible. Waiting and hoping that you will learn the material is not helpful. Before you know it, you can be behind in your work and on your way to earning a bad grade. If the teacher and the TA have been unable to help, you should consider hiring a tutor. Many high school and college students do.

## The Facts

Hiring a tutor can be a time-consuming process. In order to prepare all the important questions to ask the tutor during the interview, you need to think about what you want from the experience. The following list can help you prepare to interview potential tutors:

- Man or woman?
  Would you prefer to work with a man or a woman? In general, many students find it easier to work with someone of their own sex.

- How many hours per week?
  Before you interview tutors, you need to think about how many hours each week you will need one. Will you need 2 hours per week or 4 hours? Much of this depends on the level of the course you are taking and how much of the material you do not understand. You could begin with 2 or 3 hours per week and cut back as you learn more.

- Where will you meet or work together?
  Decide ahead of time where you want to meet and work with the tutor.
  Do you want to meet at your house or room? Do you want to meet at the
  local library or another public location?

- What is the range you will pay per hour?
  Figure out ahead of time how much you can afford to pay per hour. If you
  are in college, your school may have a tutoring center. In many cases,
  college tutoring centers are free to enrolled students or available at a very
  low cost.

If your school does not have a tutoring center, consider the guidelines below
for tutoring fees. These fees usually are based on the tutor's education
and experience.

- Will you work on a whole subject, with a book or ask the tutor to come up
  with lessons?
  Do you want to work on the subject in general or use your classroom
  book to work with the tutor? You also can ask the tutor to create your
  lessons. In most cases, you will want to work from your textbook so that
  you can ask the tutor to explain concepts that confuse you.

- How long will you need the tutor?
  Will you need the tutor for the whole semester or only for a few months
  or weeks? This is one of the first questions a tutor will ask, so you need
  to think about the answer in advance. It is possible that you will not know
  how long you want to work with the tutor. This is perfectly acceptable.

## Tutoring Fees

Tutoring fees are usually based on two factors: education and experience. As noted
before, tutors who work at colleges are often free to students or available at a
small charge. In addition, people who live in a rural area or small town will tend
to pay less for these services, while those who live in a large city or urban area will
tend to pay more.

Check the following guidelines to find the price range you may pay for freelance
tutoring services in your area:

- Education:
  - College student–$15 to $25 per hour.
  - Completed bachelors degree–$20 to $25 per hour.
  - Completed masters degree or doctorate–$25 to $35 per hour.
- Experience:
  - Teaching background in English as a Second Language (ESL)–$15 to
    $25 per hour.
  - Teaching background in high school subjects–$10 to $20 per hour.

— Teaching background in college-level subjects—$20 to $35 per hour.

## The Solutions

If you are being tutored at a tutoring center at your college, you may not be able to choose which tutor you want. However, if you are paying for a freelance tutor, you will want to interview a number of them so that you can choose the one best suited to your needs.

Ask each tutor the following useful questions and write down their answers:

How long have you been a tutor?
Ask about his or her experience as a tutor. You want someone who has tutored students before in this subject and at this level.

What is your education?
Ask about his or her level of education. You will pay more for someone with a master's degree or a doctorate. You do not necessarily need a tutor with an advanced degree, but you want one who is comfortable with the subject you are taking.

What is your teaching experience?
Most tutors have some teaching experience. Ask about this. If the tutor does not have teaching experience, ask why he or she went into tutoring?

What types of students do you tutor?
You want to know if the tutor has experience working with people who are your age and at your level. If you are a high school student, you want a tutor who has experience working with other high school students. If you are in college, you want someone who has tutored your subject before at the undergraduate level.

How do you establish a good rapport with students?
You will be working closely with your tutor, so you want someone you can talk to easily. You also want someone who will be patient and help you. This is why you need to interview potential tutors in person.

How do you view your role as a tutor?
This question is a good way to find out how a tutor will help students and what kind of a personality the tutor has.

How do you decide what each student needs help with?
You want a tutor who has patience and can explain the subject in a way that makes sense to you. You will be asking the tutor for specific help, but you also want the tutor to explain other concepts that you will need in the future.

Do you have references?
References are absolutely necessary for tutors. You want a list of three to

five names of students this person has tutored in the past.

## Working with a Tutor

Think about how you want to work with a tutor and what you will do if the tutor does not work out. Following are some tips for working with a tutor:

Check references.
> No matter who recommends the tutor to you, check his or her references. Tutors who work at colleges usually have been interviewed by instructors or administrators.

Ensure that you have good rapport.
> You need to have a good working relationship with your tutor. You should know if there is a problem after six to eight meetings. Give the tutor a little time to get used to you before you make a final decision. However, if you do not feel comfortable with your tutor or do not feel that this person is helping you, you need to find someone else.

Make sure the tutor arrives on time and leaves on time.
> Since you are paying for a freelance tutor's time, you want to hire a person who is on time and does not leave early. In addition, you want someone you can count on to be there when you schedule a tutoring session. If your tutor forgets your appointments or arrives late, consider getting a new tutor.

Set specific goals.
> The best tutoring sessions, like the best study sessions, have specific goals. Make sure to talk with your tutor about what you want to accomplish. Remember that you want to understand the material, and if you understand the material, you will be able to do well on the tests.

Find out if the tutor is encouraging and patient.
> You want a tutor who helps you and does not make you feel stupid. The tutor should be encouraging and patient in explaining the material. After a few tutoring sessions, you should feel more comfortable with the material and more confident about your knowledge of it.

## The Resources

The following resources offer more information about hiring a tutor:

*www.dso.iastate.edu/asc/tutoring/getatutor.html*
> This Website from Iowa State University offers a good FAQ section about what to expect from a tutor and what the tutor should expect from you.

*www.ams.ubc.ca/content.cfm?ID=90*
> This Website from the Alma Mater Society of the University of British Columbia has useful tips for hiring the best tutor for your needs.

# 27

# Getting Additional Help from Parents

A desperate student is trying to contact her study partner about a question that she has on her science homework. Unfortunately, her friend has not answered the cell phone or replied to instant messages or e-mails. Suddenly, it occurs to the student that her father is an engineer and her mother is a teacher.

She asks her father for advice. He seems pleased, but her mother is the one who knows the answer. In fact, her mother offers to go over a difficult chapter with her over the weekend. She never realized that her mother spent years working in a lab during graduate school.

## The Challenge

Asking parents for help with homework or other school projects can be difficult. Some students do not want to talk to their parents any more than is absolutely necessary, and others do not want their parents trying to tell them how to do the homework. No matter how you feel about them, parents can be an excellent resource for help.

One of the key tasks of adult life is time management. Your parents may be able to help you manage your time more efficiently, and they certainly can help you find a quiet place to study. However, it can be difficult to get the help of your parents when you want it, without inviting them to manage your school life the rest of the time.

## The Facts

Research has shown that parents who provide a home environment that encourages learning are giving their children the gift of achievement in school and in life. Parents who read aloud to their children, ask about schoolwork or school projects and go over homework are more important than family income, educational level or cultural background to student achievement. Students who can talk to their parents about their schoolwork or school issues are more likely to do well and go on to college.

Many students would not consider asking their parents for help with their classes. However, parents can provide you with help, advice and praise for your work. Following are several reasons to ask your parents for help with school:

- They were students once too.
- Parents can make the house quieter.
- Parents can keep younger siblings in tow.
- Parents can help you organize a project, a speech or a paper.
- Parents are a good resource for trying out your ideas.
- Parents can help proofread papers.
- Parents can be your audience when you practice a speech.
- Parents can help you study with flashcards.
- Parents can give you advice about time management.
- Parents can praise you and tell you how great you are.

## The Solutions

The difficulty with parents is that they can decide to micromanage your life if you ask them for help. The goal is to get their help without allowing them to take over. The key to this delicate balance is communication. If you explain to your parents what you need from them and then keep the lines of communication open, you should be able to get the help that you need without allowing them to schedule the rest of your life.

Several suggestions about how to get help without endless advice follow:

- Ask for what you need.
  The first step is to ask for exactly what you need–advice, guidance, quiet, etc. Be specific; if you are vague, your parents may decide that you need them to organize your entire study life instead of your research paper. For this reason, think about it ahead of time and be prepared to ask for something specific. You may even want to give them a time limit within which you will need their help.

- Tell them your study plan, research plan or other school-related plans.
  Once you have asked for and gotten help from your parents, you will need to tell them about your study plans. Telling them this information will keep them from asking you or assuming that you do not have any. Be proactive with them and explain your current studies.

  If your parents suspect that you do not have any study plans or do not understand how to organize your schoolwork, they may decide to become intimately involved. If you want to organize your own life, make them feel comfortable that you have everything under control.

- Set specific times to check in with your parents or ask them questions.
  If you need help from your parents but you are concerned about the

possibility of them taking over, consider setting up a family homework hot line. Schedule a time every night that you can ask your parents study-related questions. After that time is over, remind them that you will be studying and do not want to be disturbed. You also can ask that they keep any younger siblings quiet when you are trying to do your work.

- Keep your parents up-to-date about your progress and grades.
  Proactively update your parents about your grades. If they have helped you organize a research paper, be sure to bring it home and show them the grade. Even if you are in college, they will be pleased that they were able to help. Telling your parents in advance is an excellent way to keep them from having to ask you. If you freely provide the information, they will realize that you are capable of managing your own schoolwork.

- Do not allow your parents to pay you for good grades.
  Many students have the mistaken idea that parents or grandparents should pay them for good grades. Grades are a good example of goals that you have little control over. In high school, they are frequently about who the teacher likes or perceives to be the best student. Even good students may get only a B in some courses because the teacher grades on a curve. However, those students may have studied hours longer than the A students. If possible, ask your parents or other family members to provide rewards for you when you stick to your study schedule.

- Do not allow your parents to do your homework for you.
  Some parents are not happy unless they are doing their children's homework. Do not allow your parents to do this. If they do your homework, you will not learn anything. After all, are you planning to ask them to talk to your boss when you get your first job? Will they be dropping in to help you finish your business proposal or run the corporate meeting?

- Alert them to scheduled study groups or study partners.
  Make sure that your parents know when you will be hosting your study group or study partner. They can make a comfortable room available to you and restrict your younger siblings to their rooms. In addition, parents often feel inclined to offer snacks to help you and your friends study better. As long as your parents are not interrupting you during your quiet study time, allow them to help.

## The Resources

The following resources offer more information about asking your parents for help with school:

*www.nea.org/parents/index.html*

This Website from the National Education Association explains the research that has been done about how parents can help their children succeed in school.

*www.kidsource.com/kidsource/content/homework.html*

The advice on this Website is geared toward parents of grade school and middle school students, but the section on helping with homework applies to high school students as well.

*www.nea.org/parents/homework.html*

This page from the National Education Association's Website offers excellent insight into the purpose of homework for children from grade school through high school.

# 28

# Getting Additional Help from Friends

A junior college student is having difficulty with his math class. He has been attending class lately, but he missed a few weeks at the beginning of the semester. Because the later material built on the foundation laid down in the first weeks, he is now quite confused.

He is afraid to talk to the professor or the teaching assistant because he knows that he did not do his part. Although he has read the chapters covered during the first few weeks, he does not understand many of the concepts.

He is thinking about asking a student in another class to help him. Although the other student is in a more advanced math class, she is easy to talk with and patient.

## The Challenge

Studying alone can be a difficult task. The textbooks are long and complicated, and there is no one to talk to. Sometimes even the best students can use a break from solitary study. Moreover, some students do better when they have a group or another person to study with, especially auditory and kinesthetic learners.

## The Facts

Everyone can benefit from studying with others from time to time. Answer the following questions and be as honest as you can:

- Do you have difficulty managing your study time?
- Are you easily distracted?
- Does one or more of your classes bore you?
- Do you have too much to do and not know where to start?
- Do you need to do your homework but cannot move forward because your work has to be perfect?
- Are you afraid to study because you are concerned about test scores or test anxiety?

If you answered yes to two or three questions, you probably could benefit from studying with someone else.

## Choosing a Study Partner

Choosing a study partner or study group can be difficult. You want to choose someone you like, but sometimes the people you like are more interested in talking than working. You also want to choose someone who can agree to some ground rules so that you do not squander your study time.

The following list of personality traits will help you decide which of your friends or schoolmates would be a good candidate for a study partner:

Serious and dependable.

You want to study with someone who will spend the time studying and who will not forget your study appointments. If you study with someone who is not as serious as you are, your study partner may convince you to talk rather than study.

Likable and supportive.

A study partner needs to be likable too. It would be difficult to spend significant amounts of time with someone who is not fun to be with. Your study partner also has to be supportive of you.

Similar study goals.

While you do not have to be in the same class or even the same school to be study partners, it helps if you both have the same study goals. If your friend is more interested in social activities than academics, he or she will not be a good fit if your number one goal is to get into a really good college.

Your study goals also should include your goals for group study. What do you hope that your study partner can help you achieve? Do you need someone to talk to about ideas for your projects, papers or speeches? Do you need someone to help you remember to keep your study breaks short? Discuss your goals with your potential study partner.

Similar calendars.

You and your study partner should be able to work out a schedule. Students are so busy with work and school that trying to fit in another commitment can be difficult. However, having a specific date and time to study and a person to study with are a great motivators.

Amenable to specific dates and times.

A study partner is no help if that person will not agree to specific dates and times. Agreeing to get together at some unspecified time is insufficient. You both may forget and schedule other activities. While you probably cannot plan your study time months in advance, you need to schedule at least one or two meetings in the next week or so.

## The Solutions

### Three Choices for Study Friends

These days, students have three choices if they want to study with friends or classmates:

- They can find a study partner and meet with that person several times a week;
- they can join or create a study group and meet with that group several times a week; or
- they can create or join a virtual study environment.

Students who opt for the third choice can check in with a virtual study group or virtual study partner via instant messaging, e-mail or telephone.

The flexibility of the three choices can make your life much easier. As always, the trouble is managing your time so that you do not chat with your study friends when you should be studying.

### Ground Rules for Study Friends

Just as study groups need rules to keep them on task and on schedule, study partners need rules to make sure that work gets done. Following are several suggestions for good ground rules:

Arrive on time.
> Make sure that you both are on time for your study sessions so that you can end them on time, too. If your study partner is always late, you will know that he or she is not really serious about studying.

Agree to a study schedule and specific breaks.
> The first order of business when you meet is to set up a study schedule that includes what you will study, how long you will study it and when you get to take breaks. Make sure that the times when you begin and end breaks are clear and specific.

> Also, be specific about when you will be done studying each subject and when you will be done for the day. End on time and then do something fun as a reward for studying.

Do not interrupt each other.
> Agree not to disturb each other during the study periods. Each of you should keep a pad of paper nearby. When you think of something that you want to tell the other person, jot it down and tell them during the next break.

Do not allow the other person to interrupt or distract you. Keep music to a minimum and in the background. Do not allow your study partner to talk to someone else or play with electronics. Neither of you should reinforce the other's bad study habits.

Try not to be competitive.

Be encouraging and supportive of your study partner. Do not allow yourself to be competitive or compare class grades, scores or teacher comments.

Allow time to teach each other.

An excellent way to learn something thoroughly is to try to teach it to someone else. Allow time in your study schedule to teach each other new concepts, new information or new skills from your textbooks.

Allow time to share ideas.

Allow time in your study schedule to share project, paper or speech ideas with one another. Your study partner can help you choose a topic for your next paper, practice your speech, plan your study schedule, organize a group project or just help you talk through your ideas for research on the Internet.

Plan rewards together.

Plan rewards for yourselves if you stick to your study schedule. Go to a movie together, go out to dinner or coffee or meet your other friends for a party. You will study better and be more motivated if you allow yourself some rewards after you do your work.

## The Resources

The following resources offer more information about how to study with friends or fellow students:

*http://youth.ipswich.qld.gov.au/education/studying_with_friends. php?print=true*

This Website from the Ipswich City Council in Australia offers excellent advice about how to study with friends.

*www.cdtl.nus.edu.sg/examprep/sec4.htm*

This Website from the National University of Singapore explains how to work with a study group and why such a group is helpful for college students.

# Taking Tests & Studying with Intensity

A college student has an English test in a week, and he is a little nervous about it. He usually does well, but he has a history test the same day. This student usually can study for one test without a problem, but two tests mean twice as much work. He needs a way to do serious work without using up all of his study time because he has to divide the time between two classes.

## The Challenge

Studying diligently can be difficult, especially if you have more than one test on the same day or during the same week. Unlike exam week, test days are also class days. College students can have several tests, a speech and a paper all due during midterms or at other times in the semester.

Students need to understand how to study with intensity without wasting time. The key is to use every minute wisely.

## The Facts

Students who do not want to waste valuable study time need to carefully evaluate what will be on the test. During the test, they need to pace themselves and allow time to edit or review their answers.

- Chapters covered.
  When the test is announced, find out exactly what material will be covered. Ask your teacher or teaching assistant which chapters, which sections, which concepts and which vocabulary words will be on it.

- Type of test.
  Find out what types of questions will be on the test: multiple choice, true/false, short answer, essay, combination. Try to find out how much of the test will be objective and how much will be essay.

- How test will be graded.
  Find out how the test will be graded or the number of points it will be worth. Be sure to ask how much it will count toward your final grade in the class.

## A Word about Guessing

On most tests in college, students do not lose points for guessing. You have an excellent chance of guessing the right answer, especially on objective tests. This does not mean that you should not study. If you have studied, you will be able to recognize and distinguish between the right answer and the distracters, wrong answers that may seem plausible to students who did not study.

Follow these tips to guess the answer on an objective test if you do not know it:

- Eliminate wrong answers.

    If you do not know the correct answer immediately, try to eliminate choices. Cross out what you know is not the right answer, and make a choice from the options that are left.

- Go with your gut and do not change answers unless you are sure.

    Research shows that your first choice is right about 80 percent of the time. Do not change answers unless you are certain.

## Test Day Tips

Smart students use their test time carefully. You want to give yourself enough time to answer all the questions while allowing time to edit or review the answers. It is always a good idea to go over the test to make sure that you answered every question. If you do not know the answer, guess. You may get the right answer or partial credit.

Follow the tips below to plan your strategy for the test:

Tip 1: Data Dump 1.

As soon as you get the test, write down everything you can remember from your notes and your study on your test paper. Now you have all the information you will need to succeed on the test, and you do not have to remember it anymore.

Tip 2: Overview.

Look over the whole test before you answer a single question. You want to figure out how many questions there are and how many points each question is worth. You do not want to waste 10 minutes of valuable test time trying to answer a question that is only worth a few points.

Tip 3: Data Dump 2.

After you have looked over the test, you probably will remember even more information from your studying. Write this down on your test paper.

Tip 4: Easy questions.

Start with the easiest questions. Answer as many as you can.

Tip 5: Most points.

After you have completed the easy questions, tackle the questions that are worth the most points.

Tip 6: What to skip.

If you do not know the answer for a question immediately, skip it. You can come back to it after you have completed the rest of the test. As you answer the other questions, you may remember the correct answer.

Tip 7: Review and check.

Before you hand in the test, take a few minutes to review your answers. In addition, check to make sure that you have answered every question.

## A Word about Essay Questions

Essay questions often pose specific problems for students. Even good students tend to spend more time on them than on the objective portion of the test. This is a fine strategy if the essay questions are worth the most points. However, if they are not, a better plan is to answer all of the objective questions first and then the essay questions.

Give yourself a time limit. Outline what you want to say before you write the answer. Teachers are always pleased by neat answers that are written in the standard essay format.

Restate the question in your topic sentence and then provide examples to back it up. End by restating the topic sentence. Even if it takes you a few more minutes, answering in this format will help you earn maximum points.

## The Solutions

Students who want to be successful will begin using their time wisely at the start of the semester. If you study every week and review your notes, you will have much less work to do when a test is announced. In fact, you will have done most of the work already.

Follow the tips below to improve your study intensity:

- Semester-long habits
    Use your time wisely all semester.
- Short sessions
    Study in short bursts. Research suggests that three 20-minute study sessions are more useful than a single 1-hour study session.
- Repetition
    Repetition moves information from short-term into long-term memory. Use it to your advantage.
- Stop before bedtime
    Do not study just before bed. Stop at least 1 hour before bedtime so that you do not have nightmares about the test.

## Study Tools

The following study tools can help you study in short bursts and still remember everything you will need for the test:

Intro and conclusion of book chapters, summary and review questions.
> Use the introduction and the conclusion of your textbook to help you study. If your book includes a summary or review questions, use these to help you isolate the main concepts and vocabulary words for the test.

Outline of main points per lecture notes.
> Use your in-class lecture notes to create an outline of the main points in each chapter that will be included on the test. Take this outline with you and look at it for at least 15 minutes per day. Do this in 5-minute increments and you will remember everything you need for the test.

Timeline.
> Create a timeline if your class includes dates or periods in history. Do this from memory and then check it against your textbook. A timeline can help you to place actions in context and be successful on the test.

Notecards.
> Create flashcards based on the main points from your in-class notes and your textbook. Carry these cards with you throughout the day and look at them. Just 15 minutes per day can help you remember all the definitions and facts for the test.

Make your own test.
> Create a test of your own. Look at the chapters, vocabulary words and concepts and decide what you would ask if you were the teacher. This sort of practice is one of the best uses of your time. Keep track of how often you were right about the questions. This skill will be useful in all of your college classes.

## The Resources

The following resources offer more information about studying with intensity:

*www.teachervision.fen.com/study-skills/educational-testing/2026.html*
> This Website explains how to study before, during and after a test.

*http://academic.cuesta.edu/acasupp/as/707.htm*
> This Website from Cuesta Community College in California explains exactly how to take a test and how to get the information from your brain to the paper at test time.

*www.columbia.edu/cu/augustine/study/intense.html*
> This additional Website from Columbia College explains how to study with intensity.

# *30*
# Overcoming Test Stress

A college freshman is worried about her final examinations. She did not do well on tests in high school, and is worried that she will not do well on her exams now.

She has studied diligently over a long period of time, but she is concerned that test anxiety during each exam will hurt her scores. Although she did not exhibit physical symptoms of stress during high school, she often blanked on tests and could not remember anything.

After the test was over, she would remember the answers to all the questions that she did not complete. She is concerned that this will happen to her again.

## The Challenge

All students can find it difficult to do well on tests. Students who experience test anxiety, also called test stress, face an even tougher challenge. They are struggling against themselves as well as striving to get a good grade.

Even good students suffer from varying degrees of test stress, but there are a variety of techniques that can help them overcome this anxiety.

## The Facts

### Do You Suffer from Test Stress?

Maybe you do not think that tests bother you. To find out, answer the following questions as honestly as you can:

- Do you think that you will not do well on a test no matter how hard you study?
- Do you find that everything distracts you when you are trying to study for a test?
- Do you have a headache, an upset stomach, sweaty palms or other signs of stress while taking a test?
- Do you ever have difficulty understanding or reading the test directions or questions?

- Do you have difficulty studying for a test?
- Do you ever have problems concentrating when you are taking a test?
- Do you often get a lower grade on tests than on other assignments or homework?
- Do you ever go blank during a test and forget the correct answers?
- Do you ever have problems getting organized or pacing yourself when you are taking a test?
- Do you remember everything you needed to know after the test is over?

If you answered yes to more than two questions, you probably suffer from some level of test stress. You can use a variety of techniques to combat this anxiety, relax and remember the information that you studied.

## Myths about Test Stress

Many students with test stress think that good students never feel nervous before they take a test. That is untrue. Even good students who have studied diligently can feel nervous about taking a test. However, these students have a past history of doing well on tests that they can draw on to help them when they experience stress.

The following are other common myths about test stress:

- Getting rid of test stress will guarantee good grades.
- Smart students do not have test stress.
- Test stress will go away by itself.
- Students who study regularly do not have test stress.
- There is nothing anyone can do about test stress.

## The Solutions

While there are no simple solutions to test anxiety, experts agree that students can help themselves with a positive attitude, visualization and careful preparation. When students with test stress perform well, they are creating a history of successful test taking that will give them confidence in their abilities.

If you suffer from test stress, use the following tips before, during and after the test to help you succeed:

### Before Test

- Study over time.

    Before the test, make sure that you give yourself plenty of time to study. Studying in short bursts works best. Experts advise students with test stress to plan three study periods of 20 minutes each instead of 1 hour of continuous study.

- Keep a good attitude.

    Test stress is largely a function of negative thoughts. Thinking that you are no good at tests and that you will fail will not help you. Instead, try to maintain a positive attitude. Remind yourself that the time you spent studying will help you do well. Do not allow yourself to think negative thoughts.

- Visualize success.

   Imagine yourself doing well on the test. Imagine yourself in the room taking the test. Picture yourself with a clear mind, remembering everything that you studied. The more that you do this, the more you clearly you will be able to visualize yourself succeeding.

- Practice taking tests.

   Practice taking tests under time constraints. Create tests for yourself or join a study group. Simulate a timed test and practice your test strategies. When you are taking the real test, you will know exactly what to expect.

- Prepare your mind and body.

   Do not cram the night before a test. Instead, make sure that you get at least 8 hours of sleep for one or two nights before the test. Eat well-balanced meals and try to stay away from junk food. Caffeine and sugar will not help you be alert for the test.

   Many experts advise those with test stress to exercise before their test. This will help your muscles to stretch and be more relaxed.

## During Test

- Practice deep breathing.

   Try to relax your muscles and slow your heart rate by doing deep-breathing exercises.

- Only allow positive thoughts.

   Do not allow any negative thoughts to enter your mind while you are taking the test. You do not have time to waste on them. If you think something negative, immediately stop and concentrate on your test strategy.

- Get an overview first.

   Before you do anything else, write down all the formulas, notes or mnemonics that you can remember on the test paper. You can refer back to them when you need to. This also will help your stress level because you will no longer have to remember everything. Next, look over the entire test. Determine how many questions there are and how many points each one is worth. After you have done so, write down any other information that you can think of on your paper. Everything you need will be right there in front of you.

- Manage your time.

  Start with the easiest questions and then move on to the ones that are worth the most points. If all the questions are worth the same number of points, divide your time by the number of questions. Do not spend more time on any one question than you have allotted. Essay questions can waste a great deal of time. Be sure to watch the clock so that you do not spend too much time on them.

- Do not be distracted by others,

  Pay no attention to the other students. As far as you are concerned, they do not exist. Students who turn in their papers quickly are not necessarily the best students. Use the entire test period so that you can go back and check your answers.

## After Test

- Forget about it.

  After you have handed in your test, try to forget about it. You cannot do anything more. Reward yourself for studying and making it through. Do not bother to talk to other students about the test. Some will tell you that they did well, while others will endlessly go over the questions. Ignore them. The matter is now beyond your control.

- Look for ways to improve.

  When you get the test back, learn from your errors. Figure out why you chose the wrong answers. Did you misunderstand the directions? Were you moving quickly and making careless errors? Find out what you did wrong so that you can work harder on that aspect for the next test.

## The Resources

The following resources offer more information about dealing with test stress:

*www.parenting.com/parenting/child/article/0,19840,1155618,00.html*

This Website from *Parenting* magazine offers excellent advice for parents who are helping their children deal with test stress.

*www.studygs.net/tstprp8.htm*

This study Website offers worthwhile tips for preparing for a big test and dealing with the anxiety.

*www.petersons.com/common/article.asp?id=484&path=ug.pft. advice&sponsor=1*

This Website explains how to organize your thoughts and prepare your body to beat test stress.

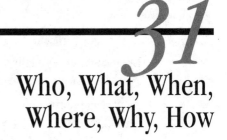

# Who, What, When, Where, Why, How

A college freshman is working on a paper for his English class. On an early draft, his professor told him that he had buried his lead. The teacher went on to explain that he had hidden the main point of his essay until the end.

The student does not quite understand what his teacher means when he tells students to write in an inverted pyramid style. Finally, the teacher explained that this meant students could use a journalistic style to find out what is really important in their essays and research papers.

## The Challenge

Too many English students do not know what the main points of their essays are or how to bring them to the forefront of their writing. Using the journalistic style of the five W's and an H can help them.

A number of English professors ask students to use the inverted pyramid style of writing. Some professors use this style because most professional and business writers use it. Others use it because most Websites are built in accordance with this style. Many instructors want their students to be more flexible in their writing and in their approach to rhetorical subjects. Whatever the reason, this journalistic style is easy to master with a little practice.

## The Facts

Most newspaper stories follow the inverted pyramid style. This style places the pyramid on its apex and begins with the most important information. It is exemplified by the following tips:

Most important points first.
In this style, the main point is presented first. Any conclusion that the writer has come to about the subject is presented in the very first line. The idea is to grab the reader's attention from the beginning. Newspaper writers want their readers to be able to skim the article or read only the first few paragraphs to figure out what the piece is about.

Supporting information and examples next.

The second block of information in every newspaper story consists of examples that support the main point or other relevant information.

Least important information last.

The last thing in the story is the least important information. If their readers actually read the whole piece, journalists want them to get all the details in the last few paragraphs.

## What Is a Lead?

In a newspaper story, the lead is the first sentence. The lead should tell the reader what the article is about and why the subject is important.

Leads can be difficult to write because the first sentence is so important. A good lead is wonderful and inevitable. It has all of the following traits:

| | |
|---|---|
| **Voice** | A good lead conveys the impression of a person talking to the reader. Readers feel as if they are in good hands. |
| **Form** | The lead allows readers to see that there is a structure or form behind the words. |
| **Context** | A good lead tells readers why they should care about your subject, your essay or your opinion. |
| **Specific focus** | The focus of a good lead lets the reader know a little of the story that follows, but only a little. |
| **Surprise** | The lead can provide a surprise to the reader with an interesting turn of phrase or two very different people or objects linked together. A bad lead often makes the whole essay clumsy and slow. It has one or more of the following traits: |
| • **Buried** | A bad lead is stuck somewhere in the third or fourth sentence of the first paragraph or the first sentence of the second paragraph. It conveys the impression that the writer only just figured out what the story is about. |
| • **Flabby or cluttered** | Leads with too many ideas or too many words are hard for readers to comprehend. In addition, they do not catch the reader's attention. |
| • **Insiders only** | Some leads use jargon that the average reader will not understand. |
| • **Boring or ho-hum** | Leads with trite words or phrases are ho-hum. Boring leads make readers tune out after just a few words and move on to the next article. |

## The Solutions

According to the journalistic style, any written work such as an article or essay should answer the following questions in order:

| Who? | Who did what to whom? This is a newspaper reporter's mantra. For many of your readers, the most important detail in your essay will be who was involved. |
|---|---|
| What? | What happened to that person or persons? What will they do or what are they about to do? |
| When? | When did this happen or when will it happen? |
| Where? | Where did this happen? Where will it happen? |
| Why? | Why did this happen? Why will it happen? |
| How? | How did this action come about? How will this action come about? |

## News Reporters' Guide to Engaging the Reader

Experts agree that the best writing engages the reader. To make sure that your readers actually care about what you write, you need to follow the four tips below:

Tip 1: News
    Include the five W's and an H–who, what, when, where, why and how– in your writing. The best place to put this information is right in the first paragraph.

Tip 2: Impact
    Explain why what you have to say is important. What is the impact of your information on the reader? Why should the reader care?

Tip 3: Context
    What is the background of your story? Is this information part of the day-to-day world, or is it out of the ordinary?

Tip 4: Emotion
    When you tell the story of a specific person, you are bringing the news to the human level. Your readers will care about what you write, and it will matter to them.

## News Reporters' Tips for Clear, Concise Writing

Newspaper reporters are known for their clear, concise writing style and their ability to create pictures with words. Students who want to bring this quality to their own writing can do so by following the tips below:

Limit ideas.
    Do not try to pack two or three ideas into each sentence. One sentence equals one idea. Simple is better.
    *Not this:*
    Since he was running for public office, Frank decided to buy a new tuxedo with a purple vest.

*But this:*
Frank bought a new tuxedo with a purple vest. He was running for public office.

Limit words.

Most newspaper writers want to keep their sentences short. In general, you do not want to write more than someone can say in one breath. Journalists agree that 20 to 25 words per sentence is the correct range.
*Not this:*
Caught in the act, the burglar was so frightened that he dropped his bag containing $100,000 in diamonds and other rare jewels and ran toward the security fence chased by guard dogs.
*But this:*
The police caught the burglar as he was leaving the house. He was chased by guard dogs and dropped a bag while running to the security gate. The bag held $100,000 in jewels.

Use subject-verb-object (SVO) construction.

Keep your writing simple and concise by using SVO construction. Do not use a number of commas or write sentences with clause after clause. Stick with a straightforward approach. Keep prepositional phrases to a minimum—no more than three of them in a sentence.
*Not this:*
Although normally he did not drink alcohol, Johnson decided to try a martini at lunch.
*But this:*
Johnson drank a martini at lunch. He normally did not drink alcohol.

Use active voice and strong verbs.

Be clear about who does what to whom. Passive sentences do not make clear who is acting.
*Not this:*
The evening paper was delivered late by Fred, the local paperboy.
*But this:*
Fred the paperboy delivered his papers later than usual.

Simplify. Simplify. Simplify.

News reporters do not have the luxury of using complex or complicated words. They want their readers to be able to understand what has happened immediately. For this reason, the journalistic style reduces cumbersome words to their simplest terms. Journalists also stay away from jargon and bureaucratic terms.

*Not this:*

Despite the delay, Mr. Johnson managed to convene the meeting in accordance with the company's minutes.

*But this:*

Mr. Johnson brought the meeting to order 5 minutes late.

## The Resources

The following resources offer more information about writing in the style of journalists:

*www.grad.ubc.ca/gradpd/guides/executivewriting.html*

Although this Website says that it is for executive writing, the authors follow the inverted pyramid style used by most journalists. The explanation of this style and the tips are excellent.

*www.media-awareness.ca/english/resources/special_initiatives/toolkit_resources/tipsheets/writing_news_story.cfm*

This Website from the Media Awareness Network offers good definitions of the journalistic style and tips for making essays interesting.

*www3.niu.edu/newsplace/j-skills-5ws.html*

This Website from Northern Illinois University offers useful tips and tricks for writing in the journalistic style.

# Study for the
# Test Format

A new student has an essay test in a week. She knows how to study for an objective test because she has studied for so many in the past, but this is her first essay test.

The student is concerned that she will overstudy and review all the wrong information. She is also uncertain about how to format her answers. Until now, she has written only essays that she could rewrite at home. She is worried that she will freeze up during the test or be unable to think of anything to write.

## The Challenge

Most students know how to study for an objective test because they have had so many during their school careers, but many take their first essay test in college. Some may have answered essay questions before, but few have written an entire essay during class.

Students must be able to study and be prepared for any kind of test, including multiple-choice, short-answer, essay, true/false, open-book or oral assessments.

## The Facts

While they have been unpopular in the past, open-book tests and oral tests are gaining acceptance.

### Open-Book Tests

As the name implies, an open-book test allows students to bring their book and use it during the test. However, doing this will only take up valuable test time. Smart students study just as they would if they could not use the book.

### Oral Tests

Oral tests are presentations that serve as tests. Usually, the teacher will meet with each student one-on-one and ask several questions. Students who can present their thoughts in a coherent and organized fashion do well on this sort of test.

To study for an oral test, students should study as they would for an essay test. In addition, students should practice explaining concepts and facts in their own words.

## The Solutions

### Objective Tests

Objective tests can include true/false, multiple-choice and sometimes short-answer questions. Some short-answer questions are more like essay questions than true objective ones.

On test day, students should use the following tips for answering true/false questions:

If any part is false, the whole sentence is false.
> In true/false items, students should remember that the entire sentence must be true.

Beware of negatives.
> Negatives such as no, not and others can be confusing. If you are uncertain about what is being stated, try to turn the sentence around and recreate it without the negatives.

Beware of qualifiers.
> Qualifiers are words such as sometimes, often, frequently and the like. Teachers use these to confuse students who may not have studied diligently.

Beware of absolutes.
> Words such as always, never and only indicate that there are no exceptions to a rule. When you see one of these words in a true/false question, look at the sentence closely to see what the absolute is referring to.

Multiple-choice questions can be tricky if there are a number of possible correct answers. These fake answers are called distracters. In order to be successful answering multiple-choice questions, students should follow the study tips below:

Facts and key concepts.
> Multiple-choice tests usually are used to test both facts and key concepts. Clever teachers will use similar distracters to trick unwary students.

Review lecture notes and book notes.
> The best way to study for multiple-choice questions is to review both your lecture notes and your book notes.

On test day, students should follow the tips below to succeed on multiple-choice tests:

Brain Dumps 1 and 2.
>Many students find it helpful to write down all their mnemonic devices on the test paper. Do this immediately after receiving your test.

Overview.
>Look over the test to get a sense of what types of questions there are. Some questions or answers can jog your memory and help you remember others.

Identify incorrect choices.
>If you do not know the correct answer immediately, try to eliminate choices. Cross out what you know is not the right answer and make a choice from the options that are left.

Go with your gut and do not change answers unless you are sure.
>Research shows that your first choice is right about 80 percent of the time.

Guess if no there is no penalty for doing so.
>If you do not lose points for guessing, you should do so.

Beware distracters that are not familiar.
>If the distracters do not look familiar, that is a clue that they do not represent correct answer choices.

## Essay Tests

Essay questions and many short-answer questions are used to test critical thinking skills and the ability to draw together concepts and make predictions about them.

### Short-Answer Questions

For short-answer questions, the following type of study aid works best:

Summary sheets.
>Use summary sheets to review for this type of item. Short-answer questions may contain factual information or be used to test critical thinking.

On test day, students should follow the tips below to succeed with short-answer questions:

Use simple sentences.
>Use simple sentences when answering short-answer questions. Use more complex constructions if the short-answer question is asking you to compare or contrast more than one item.

Fill sentences with as much information as possible.

If the short-answer question is asking for factual information, make sure to put everything you can think of into the sentence. You want to make sure that you get complete points.

### Essay Questions

Essay questions can be complicated because many students have never answered them on tests before. Even fewer have had a test with only essay questions on it. However, essay tests are no more difficult than any other type of test.

Students should follow the tips below to study for essay items:

Look at overview of material.

Essay questions usually ask students to use their critical thinking skills. Students may be asked to compare or contrast various concepts or ideas. The best way to study for this type of question is to take a global view of the materials as you review your notes. Essay questions usually require examples to back up the answers rather than facts.

On test day, students should follow the tips below to succeed with essay questions:

Jot down outline of main points.

Give yourself a time limit on essay questions. Outline what you want to say before you write the answer. Restate the essay question in your topic sentence. Put examples in support of your point into the middle.

Neatness counts.

Make sure to write neatly when answering essay questions. The teacher may have to read hundreds of essays, so make sure that yours will not strain his or her eyes.

## The Resources

The following resources offer more information about studying for tests in different formats:

*www.usu.edu/arc/idea_sheets/*

This Website from Utah State University provides test and study strategies for every kind of test.

*www.ucc.vt.edu/stdysk/stdyhlp.html*

This Website explains how to be more successful when you are taking tests or studying for them. You can download their mini-class on seven strategies for taking tests.

# Review Tools for Tests

A part-time graduate student has her first big test next week. She is trying to gather all of her review materials together, but she does not know what she should study for the test.

She also is concerned about how she will do. Back in high school, she used to get very anxious before tests. Quizzes did not bother her, but big tests or finals were always a problem.

The student thinks that she will feel less nervous if she reviews carefully and learns how to take a test. She knows that there is some kind of strategy for taking tests, but she does not know what it is.

## The Challenge

Every student needs to know how to study for and succeed on tests. Along with papers and projects, tests are one of the three major methods of ascertaining a student's success. If they do not know how to take or study for tests, students will have difficulties in college.

## The Facts

One successful strategy for taking a test is method called DETER. Each letter of this word stands for a different way of looking at a test before actually taking it. Like reading a college textbook, taking a college test requires a little advance scanning.

The following is an overview of how the DETER method can help you improve your test-taking skills:

### Directions

When you get the test, do not begin to answer any questions immediately. First, read over the directions slowly. Do you understand what you are being asked to do? If you do not understand, ask your teacher to explain. If you do not follow the directions correctly, you will not succeed on the test.

### Examine

Now scan the entire test. You need to know how many questions there are and how many total points they are worth. With this information, you will be able to figure out how much time to spend on each section. As you look over each section of the test, take note of what you are required to answer. Scanning first gives your brain time to find where the information is stored and bring it back from long-term into short-term memory.

### Time

Plan to spend most of your time on the questions worth the highest number of points. If all the questions are worth the same number of points, you can divide the time you have left evenly among all the questions.

Essay tests can be difficult to finish on time, so make sure to keep track of how much time you have allowed for each question and how much time remains.

### Easy

Answer the easiest questions first and then move on to the ones that will earn you the most points. If you start on an item and do not know the answer immediately, move on. You may think of the answer as you are answering another question.

### Review

After you have answered all the questions, take a few minutes to look over your answers one more time. Make sure that you are following the directions correctly and that you have answered every question.

If you are using a standardized answer sheet that you fill in with a pencil, take special care to make sure that you did not skip a row and mark answers to the wrong questions.

## The Solutions

### Analyze Old Tests

One way to make sure that you are studying the right information is to look at your old tests. Figuring out what you did wrong on each one will help you be more successful on the next test.

Follow the tips below to improve your test scores by looking at your earlier mistakes:

- Look over old test.
   Read any comments from the teacher and then compare your answers to the correct answers.

- Try to figure out why you got each question wrong.

  Where you unprepared for the test and did not choose the correct answer? Did you not read the question carefully and make a careless mistake?

  Look at the kind of questions you missed. Did they involve facts, figures or dates? Did they involve main points, major concepts or critical thinking? This information will help you decide what to study for the next test.

  How many questions on the old test were from the lecture, and how many were from the book? These numbers can tell you the approximate relationship of lecture to book questions for the upcoming test.

- Did you experience test stress?

  Do you remember how you felt taking the test? Did you feel anxious or upset? Did your test anxiety influence your answers or your score? If it did, you can practice relaxation techniques for test day.

### How to Create Review Tools

Students can use the notes that they already have to create study tools for tests. If you have been keeping up with the assigned reading and attending class, you should be able to use your in-class notes, your reading notes and any handouts from the teacher to help you review for the test.

Use the following tips to create useful study guides for the test:

- In-class notes

  Your in-class lecture notes can be the most useful study guide of all. Research shows that teachers usually include more questions about their lectures than information from the book on tests. For this reason, your in-class notes can be an invaluable tool for review.

  Write a summary of each page of your in-class notes or of the entire lecture for that day. In the margin, note any correlations with pages in your textbook, lab information or main ideas. Feel free to mark the most important ideas with symbols, different colored highlighters or different colored pens.

  If you have been reviewing your notes regularly for the whole semester, you should be able to review your notes for the chapters on the test quickly. When you feel comfortable with all the main points that are covered, you can create a set of study summaries or flashcards.

- Reading notes

  Your reading notes will be the second most important tool for your test review. If you have been reading and taking notes all semester, either you will have taken separate notes from your reading, or you will have highlighted your textbook and written notes in the margin. If you do not have separate reading notes, make sure to write down all the main points from your textbook. Otherwise, indicate the main points in your written notes with color or symbols. Use your notes or the textbook to create a summary sheet or flashcards to help you study for the test.

- Vocabulary

  If your class includes a large number of vocabulary words or definitions, you already may have created a vocabulary list to help you remember them. If you have not done this yet, use your lecture and reading notes to assemble one. If your book has a glossary in the back, this will make your work easier. The best method for studying vocabulary words is to create flashcards.

- Summary sheets

  Summary sheets, also called crib sheets, are just a collection of the main ideas you need to know for the test. Put this information on loose-leaf sheets or in one notebook so that you can carry the information with you easily and study without having to bring along a heavy textbook.

## The Resources

The following resources offer more information about creating review tools for a test:

*www.und.edu/dept/ULC/study/finalprep.html*

This Website from the University of North Dakota's University Learning Center offers good advice about how to review and study for final examinations.

*http://studentaffairs.case.edu/education/resources/onepagers/*

This study Website from Case Western Reserve University offers summaries of many study topics, including improving test scores in college.

*www.studygs.net/tstprp5.htm*

This Website has excellent tips for creating review tools for any kind of test.

# How to Prepare for a Math Test

A liberal arts student is worried about her upcoming math test. She has done reasonably well in her other subjects, but math is difficult for her. She feels that the other students in the class are smarter than she is.

The student does not always understand what the professor says during class, but she has a good teaching assistant. Her TA explains the material in a way that she understands and helps her with the difficult formulas.

The TA has given everyone a review sheet for the test, but the student still is concerned that she may not be studying correctly for a math test. She has been approaching her work as if she was going to take a history exam.

## The Challenge

Many excellent all-around students have difficulty with math. Because the textbook information involves problem solving and complex formulas, students do not always know how to study for a math test. They must understand the formulas, main points and the reasons behind every concept. In addition, students must be able to solve specific types of problems on the test.

## The Facts

### Before the Test is Assigned

Students need to follow up on their math studies every day. Because math builds on the foundations of earlier classes and concepts, students cannot afford to skip even a week of review or practice.

Follow the tips below to succeed on a math test:

- Do homework
  In a problem-solving class such as math, students need to do their homework every night in order to practice solving the problems. Since some problems from the homework probably will appear on the test, students are in fact studying by completing their homework.

- Make lists

     While you are doing your homework and reading your textbook every week, keep a list of vocabulary terms and concepts that you do not understand. Take this list with you to class and ask your TA or professor to help you understand them. If you decide to get a tutor, you can use this list to help you study for the test.

- Ask questions

     Ask questions whenever you have an issue or a problem with the material. You may fall behind if you do not get your questions answered immediately. Because math builds on previous lessons, if you did not understand a section earlier in the textbook, you will be unable to understand the problems that come later.

## After the Test is Announced

After the teacher announces the test and the date, make sure to get all the information about what you will need to study. Follow the tips below to help you prepare:

What will be covered?

     Make sure to ask the teacher or TA what will be covered on the test. Be sure that you know all the chapters and the concepts that will be covered. If possible, get a study guide or ask if the TA will hold a review session.

Create a study list.

     Use the information from the teacher, any review guides and your textbook to make a list of all the chapters, concepts and terms you will need to know for the test. Create a schedule to help you organize your study time. Make sure to devote enough time to the concepts that you do not understand and the types of problems that you find most difficult.

Choose example problems for each topic on the list.

     Review old homework, any workbooks for the class and the textbook and identify example problems for every topic on your study list. Practice these problems so that you will be comfortable and confident on the test.

Include many problems of all types.

     Make sure to choose every type of problem for your review session. Include story problems, distance problems and any word problems that you have been assigned. In addition, try to find easy, medium and difficult problems to complete for every topic. Solving all of these problems will help you feel relaxed and prepared for the test.

# The Solutions

## Studying for a Math Test

Studying for a math test is different than studying for any other subject. Not only do students have to understand concepts, main ideas and definitions, they also have to be able to demonstrate their knowledge by solving various kinds of problems and showing their work.

Follow the tips below to successfully study for your math test:

Tip 1: Analyze homework errors.
First, go over your homework sheets and look for the errors that you made. They will tell you what you need to spend time studying for the test. Be alert for careless errors such as not following directions or not showing your calculations. If you notice a pattern of mistakes, try to find out what concept or type of problem is giving you difficulty.

Tip 2: Go over each topic in order.
Make sure that you study each topic in the correct order. Math uses earlier skills as a foundation for teaching skills later in the semester. You also need to understand the underlying concepts in order to complete the practice problems. Be sure to devote enough study time to each topic. You will not need to spend as much studying or reviewing easy sections as you will difficult ones.

Tip 3: Review notes.
Review your in-class and reading notes. Highlight or underline the main points with colored pens or mark them with symbols such as stars, exclamation points and asterisks.

Tip 4: Practice problems.
Solve your practice problems only after you understand each concept in every topic. You will need to be able to show your work and explain how you came to each answer.

Tip 5: Create practice tests.
Create practice tests based on your work with the practice problems. Use problems that you found difficult.

Tip 6: Do problems out of order.
Make sure to solve the problems out of order as you draw closer to the test. The teacher will not put the problems in the order that the concepts appear in the textbook, so you should not practice them that way.

Tip 7: Time yourself.
Time yourself so that you will be able to organize your time during the

test. Many students do not have a test-taking strategy, and this hurts their chances of success.

## On Test Day

Write formulas down immediately.

When you get your test paper, write down every formula and fact that you memorized for the test. The information from this brain dump will help you complete all the difficult problems. You also may want to do another brain dump after you have looked over the test. The test questions may remind you of additional information.

Overview first.

Look over the entire test. See how many problems there are and what each problem is about. Determine how many points will be awarded for each question. Organize your time so that you will be able to complete the test and check your work.

Start with the easiest problems first.

Begin with the problems that you find easiest and then move on to the problems that are worth the most points. Skip problems that are giving you trouble.

Use entire period.

Use the entire time allotted for the test. Do not be distracted if other students finish before you do. Completing the test quickly does not ensure success. Remember that slow and steady often wins the race.

Check answers and proofread.

After you have answered every question, go back and check your answers. Make sure that you followed the directions correctly. Show all of your work. In math, you may receive points for using the proper formula even if you do not have the correct answer.

## The Resources

The following resources offer more information about studying for a math test:

*http://euler.slu.edu/Dept/SuccessinMath.html*

This Website from Saint Louis University has everything a math student needs to be successful studying for or taking a test.

*www.sinclair.edu/stservices/edu/Tutorial/skills/prepmath/index.cfm*

This Website from Sinclair Community College offers excellent study tips for every subject including math.

*www.mathpower.com/tip4.htm*

This Website offers 10 good suggestions for success in math class as well on math tests.

# Test Yourself

A graduate student has joined a study group to help her succeed in her classes and overcome her test stress. The group has studied together and quizzed each other. Now that a test has been assigned, they will meet in a week to do a pretest.

Each student is supposed to bring 10 questions for the pretest. They are supposed to think of questions that they would ask if they were the teacher. The student is a little confused because she has never tested herself before. She has studied but has never tried to come up with her own test questions. She thinks this is a good way to study, but she does not know where to begin.

## The Challenge

Active learning requires students to be responsible for their own learning. Part of this task can be made easier if students learn to think like teachers. Students who can come up with their own test questions and correctly guess what the teacher will ask are learning a useful skill.

Although writing your own pretest is not the only way to test yourself, many study groups use this technique to help members succeed on tests. This method is especially useful for final examinations that cover material from the entire semester.

## The Facts

Students can learn to anticipate test questions with a little practice and some insight into what concepts, facts and main points are most important. Some teachers add difficult questions that are not about the main points. However, most teachers telegraph the test questions in their lectures, notes or comments.

Smart students look for the following hints in the week or so after the teacher announces the test date:

Hint: Teacher study guide or review period.

Some teachers provide a study guide for tests, or they offer to schedule a review session for any interested students. If your teacher offers either of these options, take advantage of them. They are the ideal ways to find out what the teacher thinks is important for the test.

Hint: Teacher admission.

Many teachers will not offer information about the test, but they will answer questions. Be sure to ask about the main concepts in each chapter. Ask if the test will feature more questions from the notes or from the book. Also, ask about possible essay questions and see if the teacher will offer an example of the type of essay questions he or she usually chooses. If possible, ask the teacher to discuss how long students should study for the test and what sections are especially important.

Hint: Other clues.

If your teacher will not answer questions about the test or provide review materials, you can still find out what he or she may ask on the test. After a test is announced, most teachers inadvertently telegraph their intentions. Anything that the teacher repeats more than once probably will be on the test. Anything that the teacher writes or has previously written on the board probably will be on the test. Teachers do not bother to write down large amounts of information unless they are important.

## The Solutions

Students can test themselves in a variety of ways, limited only by their creativity. These self-tests are typically more successful if they can be done in a group. Your study partner or study group will think of items that may have slipped your mind.

Following are several ways that students can test themselves:

### Create Test Questions

Create questions based on the material that will be covered on your test. Base most of your questions on the main points, but create some more difficult questions as well. If you were going to ask the hardest possible question about the material, what would it be? Chances are that your teacher may do this as well.

### Explain Chapters or Concepts to Your Study Partner or Study Group

Explain one or more chapters to your study partner or study group. You learn something more thoroughly when you teach it to someone else. In fact, some people have said that teaching is learning in reverse. Test yourself by explaining the main ideas and concepts to someone else in your own words.

## Concept Map for the Chapters

If you are a visual learner, you may prefer to create a concept map of all the information you know about the material being covered by the test. A concept map, also called a mind map or idea map, visually represents everything you know about a subject.

There are a variety of ways to create this concept map. Some people use a chalk or dry erase board. Others use unlined sheets of paper and a pencil. Still others start with a pencil and then add color to help them remember all of the interrelationships. A concept map is usually a number of circles with lines connecting them. Begin by drawing a circle in the center of a sheet of paper. Write the most important idea or concept in it using only phrases or single words; you do not have to write in sentences. Write other important words or concepts around the main circle. Draw circles around them too. Draw lines linking the concepts that go together or have a cause-and-effect relationship.

This is a stream-of-consciousness project. Do not spend a great deal of time contemplating what you will write. Write the words that come to mind and circle them. Draw lines and arrows to indicate how these ideas are related. Erase as you need to. Often, you may need to redraw a circle closer to another key concept. Use highlighters or ink to color-code different concepts or ideas.

Once you have a framework, you can stop and rethink your work. Move things around and add more information. Continue working outward until you have listed everything you can think of that may be included on the test. This concept map is a snapshot of all you know about this subject.

## Complete Summary of Test Materials

Create a long, written summary of all the information that will be on the test. Do this in your own words after you have reviewed all the materials and your notes. Include the most important facts and vocabulary words as well as the main points, concepts or theories. Creating this summary from memory will be an excellent test of your knowledge.

## Outline

Make a list and outline of all the material from memory. Start with all the dates, vocabulary words and other facts you can remember. Do this after you have completed a review of all the materials, your in-class lecture notes, your book notes and any flashcards or summary sheets that you have created. Add the concepts, theories and main points. List any supporting information under the relevant main points or concepts. Draw lines and arrows to indicate which ideas are related to which facts or definitions.

You also need to put everything in order. You might use date order for a history class or cause-and-effect order for a science class. If your materials contain categories or other organizational methods, use them to put all of your separate thoughts together into one outline of the whole.

### Make a Game of It

Make a game of testing yourself. Use your index cards to quiz yourself in a way that is fun. You can make a quiz where you are given the answer and have to come up with the question. You can organize your game like the television shows that give away cash prizes. Obviously, this method will work best with a study group or at least two study partners.

## The Resources

The following resources offer more information about testing yourself before a test:

*http://sch.ci.lexington.ma.us/~cbruckman/testtaking*

This Website from Clark Middle School has excellent suggestions for studying any kind of material. The practice test at the end is most important.

*www.utexas.edu/student/utlc/lrnres/handouts/1445.html*

This Website from the University of Texas at Austin explains how to study for every kind of test and includes some sample objective tests at the end.

*www.wm.edu/deanofstudents/forms/AcademicCompass.pdf*

This .pdf from the College of William and Mary's Academic Skills Program offers insight into how to test yourself in a variety of ways so that you will be ready for the test.

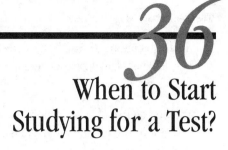

# When to Start
# Studying for a Test?

A college sophomore has a test in 2 weeks. Since he has so much time to prepare, he is in no hurry. He believes that he does his best work under pressure. Also, he does not like to study during the day and feels that he can concentrate better late at night or after he has gone out with friends.

He plans to cram the night before the test. He is usually successful when he does this, even though he has not had much sleep.

## The Challenge

Studying for tests is not easy. Even the best college students have been known to procrastinate. However, if you make studying a normal part of your school week, preparing for a test is only a review of the material you have already learned. Students should begin studying for the test on the very first day of the class and keep up with their reading, in-class notes and homework.

## The Facts

### Sleep Deprivation

Unfortunately, many students are like the student described above. They believe that they do their best work at odd hours and think that cramming for a test is the best way to prepare. Research shows, however, that most people do not do their best work under pressure. The time crunch almost always causes more test stress.

Research shows that students who sleep 8 to 9 hours a night actually do better on tests than those who cram. In fact, studies show that students who stay up for 19 or more consecutive hours lower their test performance as much as if they had a blood alcohol level of 0.1 percent. Staying up all night and then taking a test makes about as much sense as taking a test when you are legally intoxicated.

In addition, cognitive research studies indicate that college students who only get enough sleep 1 out of every 3 nights are in fact physically and mentally fatigued.

Although they are physically tired, they may feel fine emotionally. Their brains may tell them that they are operating at peak efficiency, but their academic skills are impaired.

You best course of action before a test is to study for 1 or 2 hours during the day and give your body and mind enough sleep at night.

## The Solutions

Students should start studying at the beginning of the semester. They should review their in-class and reading notes every week. If students have attended all their classes, taken notes and done all the reading, they can begin to review as soon as the test date is announced.

In most cases, test dates are listed on the class syllabus. Most students need 1 to 2 weeks to study for a test. If the class much more difficult than your others, you may need as many as 3 weeks.

If you study and review your notes every week, you are already about 60 percent ready for your test. All you have to do is review the notes to move the information from your short-term into your long-term memory.

Use the following tips to help you study for the test:

Tip 1: Create a schedule.

Create a schedule as soon as the teacher announces the test date. List everything that you need to study for the test including all facts, dates, vocabulary words and definitions. Add the major concepts and ideas that you need to know and which chapters or sections of your textbook will be included.

Schedule the time so that you will be able to review all of the materials before the actual test date and so that you will not be studying one concept without being able to revisit it again before the test. Do a general review of all the material the day before the test.

Tip 2: Study every day.

Include time for study every day in your schedule. Repetition will help you remember everything on the day of the test. It is easiest to practice repetition for short stretches over a long period. List exactly what concepts, sections or chapters you will study every day.

Also, include time to go over flashcards, summary sheets and other notes as well as reviewing your textbook.

Tip 3: Study for short periods.

Research has shown that studying for shorter periods is more effective than studying for hours. In general, three study sessions of 20 minutes each are better for college students than studying for 1 continuous hour.

Schedule time to study different chapters and different concepts on the same day. You will learn better by studying different parts of the same subject. If you try to spend all of your time on just one chapter, you may become bored or unable to concentrate. However, if you allow yourself to study several different sections, you will be able to cover more of each chapter.

Tip 4: Have a goal for each study session.

Make sure that you set time and completion goals for each day of study. Setting goals will ensure that you review all of the material before the test. Spend the most time on the concepts that are the most difficult. Save the sections that you find easy until the end. You probably already know them.

Plan study breaks as part of your goals. You may find it difficult to study without taking breaks.

Tip 5: Reward yourself for keeping your study schedule.

Just as you do in your normal study routine, you need to plan rewards when you keep to your study schedule. You can take a few minutes to play a video game, call a friend or check your e-mail. After you have completed your study for the day, you may want to give yourself bigger rewards. You can go out to dinner with your study group or your study partner.

Save the biggest rewards for when you keep to your study schedule for 1 week or more. Buy yourself a new item of clothing, a new book or some new music. Rewards are what keep most college students motivated.

Tip 6: Test yourself.

Use practice tests or other methods to test yourself. You can create test questions and answer them. You can recite the answers to help you remember them better.

You also can write a long summary or an outline of all the information that will be on the test. Do this in your own words after you have reviewed all the materials and your notes. Include all the most important facts and vocabulary words as well as the main points, concepts or theories. Creating this summary from memory will be excellent practice for the test.

Explain the chapters that will be on the test to a sibling, parent or study partner. You learn something more thoroughly when you teach it to someone else. Test yourself by explaining the main ideas and concepts to someone else in your own words.

You also can create a game to test yourself. Use any game format that you like. You can use a format where you are given the answer and have to say the question. You can organize your game like the television shows that give away cash prizes. Use your flashcards and summary sheets to test yourself, your study partner or your study group members.

You also can use a concept map to show everything that you know on the subject in a visual snapshot. Write the most important concept for the test on a blank sheet of paper. Circle it and write other important words or concepts around the main circle. Draw circles around them too. Draw lines linking the concepts that go together or have a cause-and-effect relationship.

Once you have a framework, you can add vocabulary words, definitions and facts. Continue moving outward on the sheet of paper until you have listed everything you think might be included on the test.

## The Resources

The following resources offer more information about when to begin studying for tests and how to study:

*www.studygs.net/mapping/mapping.htm*

This Website explains how students can use mind mapping, also called concept mapping, to help them summarize information for a test.

*www.studygs.net/tstprp5.htm*

This page offers review tips and tools for studying.

*http://studytips.aac.ohiou.edu/?Function=Exam*

This Website from Ohio University outlines how to prepare for any examination.

# 37

# Frequently Misused Words & Phrases

A science major is having trouble with an English class. She is supposed to write an essay, but she is not feeling motivated. She thinks that she is not getting a fair grade from her teacher. She always earned A's and B's in English classes in high school.

On every paper, the teacher points out words that the student has misused as well as words that are redundant. She would like to learn how to use these words correctly, but she has no idea where to begin. Until the teacher pointed it out to her, she did not realize that she was using them incorrectly.

## The Challenge

Many students have trouble with confusing word pairs or redundancy. Some of the difficulty is a lack of reading, and the rest probably can be attributed to e-mail, instant messaging and a lack of writing practice in most high school English classes.

## The Facts

In general, there are three types of misused words and phrases: commonly confused words, redundant phrases and trite phrases.

Following are descriptions of the three types:

> Type 1: Commonly confused words
> These are words that are similar in sound or spelling. Because of their similarity, the words are often used in place of one another.

> Type 2: Redundant phrases
> These are words or phrases that are not needed to make sense of a sentence or phrase.

> Type 3: Trite phrases
> Trite phrases, also called clichés, are words or phrases that have been overused. Once they were new and interesting ways to express an idea.

Unfortunately, they have been used so much over the years that they have little meaning now.

# The Solutions

Look at the following words and phrases. Choose those words that you often misuse, and start a list. As you write essays and research papers, you can edit out these words from your papers in the proofreading stage:

## Commonly Confused Words

A lot/allot

> A lot is always written as two words. It means many, but is often overused in student papers. Allot means to divide something up into segments or portions. For example: Trudy had a lot of homework. She decided to allot her science homework to the end of her study time.

Accept/except

> Accept means to receive something. Except means to leave something out. For example: Fred accepted his place as the CEO of the company. He wanted everyone except Fran to remain on the board of directors.

Affect/effect

> Affect is a verb that means to influence something or someone. Effect is a noun that means results. As a verb, effect means to accomplish. For example: Sheila tried to affect the election by running a last minute radio advertisement. The effect of Sheila's ad was negligible.

Assent/ascent

> Assent means to agree with something or someone. Ascent means that something or someone is climbing or has climbed to a new height. For example: George nodded his assent to the new tax cuts for his shareholders. Sandra made her ascent to the top of the mountain and called her children at home.

Complement/compliment

> Complement can be a noun or a verb. In either case, it means to complete something or make it perfect. Compliment also can be a noun or a verb, but it means to praise someone or something. For example: Jeannie complimented Fred on his good taste after he removed Fran from the board of directors. She said that Fred's new appointee, Virginia, was a better complement to the other board members.

Could of/could have

> Could have means that something had a possibility of coming true or coming to pass. It often is used as a contraction as in could've. Could of is a mispronunciation of could've. This phrase should never be used in written work. The same rule applies to should have or should've. The

phrase should of is an inappropriate usage of should have. For example: I could have gotten a new Xbox® or a new iPod. Even though I could've bought the game player, I made the right choice because I listen to music when I study.

Its/it's

Its is a possessive that means something belongs to someone. It's is a contraction of it is. For example: It's my opinion that Virginia is not qualified to be on the board of directors, but every dog has its day.

Lie/lay

Lie means to lie down. Only people or animals can lie down. However, only people can tell lies. Lay means to lay an object down. For example: Frida was going to lie down because she was feeling sick. She laid her office keys on the bedside table.

Lose/loose

Lose is a verb that means to misplace something or to fail to win a contest. Loose is an adjective that describes something that is baggy or not tight. For example: Jane was sure she would lose the race for town council. Her pants were so loose that they fell down around her ankles as she stood up to give a speech.

Principal/principle

Principal can be an adjective that means most important or a noun that means a person with authority in a certain situation. Principle is a noun that means a truth or moral code that someone may have. For example: The principal of the Do-Nothing Corporation had no principles about behaving in an unethical manner.

Stationary/stationery

Stationary means standing still or not moving. Stationery is writing paper or fancy notes. For example: My doctor told me to ride a stationary bike for 20 minutes every day for my health. My sister always buys me stationery for my birthday.

Suppose/supposed to

Suppose means to make a guess about something. Supposed to is a verb that means a person is obligated to do something. Students who use the construction suppose to have misunderstood that the -ed is required. For example: I suppose that I must attend the party at the Hilton, but I am supposed to have dinner with my family.

Than/then

Than is a word used in comparisons between two people or objects. Then means next or something that will happen at a specific time. For example: Pam is taller than Alex. We will go to the pool and then to the sauna.

To/too/two

> To is a preposition that means going toward something. Too means also or over much. Two is a number. For example: Two college students went to a party at a sorority house and drank too much beer.

Who/which/that

> Who is a pronoun that refers to one or more people. Which is a pronoun that usually indicates a question about a specific thing. Which is never used to refer to people. That is used to refer to a thing or a group of people. For example: Who did you invite to the dance? Which one is she? Oh, that one?

Your/you're

> Your is a possessive that means that something belongs to the person you are addressing. You're is a contraction of you are. For example: Your boss may be an idiot, but you're not responsible for him.

## Redundant Phrases

The following phrases are not needed to make sense of a sentence. For example, true facts is redundant because the definition of the word fact is something that is true.

- any and all
- true facts
- basic fundamentals
- period of time
- each and every
- if and when
- first and foremost

## Trite Words and Phrases

The following words and phrases are trite because they have become overused. In fact, they have been used so often that they now have little meaning to most people. Many of these phrases are acceptable in spoken English, but not in written work.

- sadder but wiser
- rat race
- learned a lesson the hard way
- at the drop of a hat
- in a nutshell
- get this show on the road
- spread like wildfire

# The Resources

The following resources offer more information about words and phrases that students commonly mix up:

*www.georgiasouthern.edu/~writingc/handouts.htm*

> This amazing Website from Georgia Southern Writing Center has quizzes, worksheets and information about everything students need to improve their writing assignments.

*http://businesswriting.com/tests/wordpairs.html*

> This Website offers an online quiz of commonly confused words.

# 38

# 10 Quick Steps
# to a Research Paper

A junior high student has to write a research paper for his English class, but he has never written one before. Until now, his teachers have spent most of their class time talking about grammar.

The student does not know where to begin. His teacher has explained the process in class, but he still does not quite understand it. He knows that he needs to find a topic, research it and write a paper, but he is unclear about how to get from one stage to the next.

He wishes that his school had a writing lab or an online writing center so that he could find out how to begin his work.

## The Challenge

Tackling a research paper is a daunting task. Most college students are familiar with writing essays, but few have written a full-blown research paper before. Students who have are at a distinct advantage over their contemporaries because they understand the overall process. Half of the difficulty of writing that first research paper is trying to understand the process while completing it. However, by the time most college students graduate, they are expert researchers and capable writers.

## The Facts

Students who write research papers often spend considerably more time doing research than writing the paper. Nevertheless, students need to remember that a research paper is primarily an essay. Students should follow the tips below to make sure that their research paper includes all the important parts of the basic essay structure:

- Introduction paragraph
  The introduction paragraph is the first paragraph of the essay. It should end with a thesis statement that tells readers what the paper is about and what the writer is trying to prove.

- Conclusion paragraph

  The conclusion paragraph is the last paragraph of the essay. It is the writer's last chance to make his or her point. The conclusion paragraph usually opens with a summary of the thesis statement and then makes the writer's final observations on the subject.

- Body paragraphs

  The paragraphs in the middle form the body of the essay. These paragraphs support the major points noted in the thesis statement. In a classic essay, there are only three body paragraphs. In a research paper, students can have as many as they need to prove their points.

- Footnotes, endnotes and in-text references

  Students need to find out how their instructor wants them to list the citations in their papers. Some teachers prefer endnotes with all of the footnotes gathered at the end of the paper. Some teachers want footnotes at the end of each page. A very few instructors want their students to include all of their citations within the body of the paper.

## The Solutions

Writing a research paper is similar to writing a long essay, except this type of paper requires references. The process is easy to follow once students understand the overall structure. To create a good research paper, students need to follow the 10 tips below:

Tip 1: Choose an appropriate topic.

One of the hardest parts of writing a research paper is choosing a topic. Even if students know what they are interested in researching, it can be difficult to narrow the topic to something that can be covered in 10 to 15 pages. If a topic is too broad, the student could write volumes about it. If the topic is too narrow, the student will be lucky to find any research at all.

For example, the symbolism of water in Emily Bronte's works is too big a topic to be covered in a short research paper. However, if the symbolism were limited to Emily Bronte's novel, *Wuthering Heights*, the topic would be an appropriate size.

Choose a topic that you find interesting. The process of creating a research paper can take 3 to 6 weeks, depending on the topic chosen and the length of the assignment.

Tip 2: Begin the research process.

Students who have narrowed their topics are ready to start researching. Starting in a college library is the best way to begin. Look up everything you can find about your topic. Be sure to read any academic journal articles on the subject and any book chapters that deal with it.

In addition, do a search on the Internet to find out if any Websites have information about this topic. For example students might look at Websites for colleges or universities if they have chosen a literary topic such as the one described above. The best Websites for this kind of topic are those created and maintained by faculty members or graduate students. Information from these sources is more likely to be accurate.

Tip 3: Keep careful records.

To avoid committing plagiarism, keep careful records of every source you consider. Students should create a research log and list every URL, book, article or chapter that they consult. They also should include authors, titles, page numbers and any Web or Internet information about each source.

If a question about plagiarism arises, students can trace every source used for their papers.

Tip 4: Create notecards.

At this stage, students need to create notecards of all the information they are researching. One set of cards should contain the bibliographical information about every source they plan to use in the paper. This set must be kept meticulously so that every detail of every source is recorded. When students start to write their papers, they will need to be certain that the correct pages are referenced in each citation.

Another set of notecards should include all of the notes students have written about their research sources. In this set of cards, they should keep track of which information is a direct quote and which is just a summary or paraphrase. Some students write down only quotations on their notecards. They know that every card contains a quotation, and they can paraphrase as much as they need to for their paper.

Tip 5: Create an outline.

The next step is for students to create an outline of their paper. They know the topic, and now they should be able to assemble all of their notes to come up with a structure.

First, create a thesis statement. A thesis is the main idea of your paper. This narrows the topic and creates an arguable point about it.

Then, construct order out of all the notecards and research information. Many students opt for an organization that starts with the weakest point in their argument and then builds to their strongest point.

Tip 6: Write the rough draft of your paper.

Once the outline is written, students need to write the rough draft of their papers. The primary purpose of this draft is to get the student's ideas written down or into a computer. Drafts can be edited if they are too long.

It is more difficult to add information if the draft is too short.

Tip 7: Revise your paper.

Once the paper is written, students should wait 1 or 2 days and then read the paper again. If students give themselves time away from their draft, they will be able to see quickly what to revise in their paper.

Tip 8: Check references and citations.

Once the paper has been revised into a second draft, students should check the references and citations one more time to be sure that they are giving credit for every idea, quotation or paraphrase from someone else's work.

Tip 9: Create a bibliography.

Once the citations have been checked for a final time, students can create the bibliography. This is a list that includes every source that the student used in the paper. Some English instructors want their students to make a two-part bibliography. A works cited section includes every source that the student referenced in the paper. A works consulted section includes every source that the student looked at while researching the paper.

Tip 10: Proofread the paper and do a final check.

Once the final bibliography has been created and edited, students can start the final check of the paper. First, the paper needs to be proofread for any spelling errors and problems with punctuation or grammar. Then, students need to create a title page that lists their name, the date, the teacher's name and the number of the course.

## The Resources

The following resources offer more information about how to write a research paper:

*www.georgiasouthern.edu/~writingc/handouts.htm*

This Website from the University Writing Center of Georgia Southern University offers information about writing a research paper along with many handouts and worksheets on grammar, sentence structure and punctuation.

*www.collegeboard.com/student/plan/college-success/10358.html*

This Website from the College Board has excellent examples of all the steps in creating a paper. The discussions of paper structure and structuring an argument are excellent.

*www.ipl.org/div/aplus/step1.htm*

This Website from the Internet Public Library for Teens includes everything students need to know about writing a research paper.

# 39

# Writing Techniques

A part-time student has to write a paper for her English class, but she does not know where to begin. The paper is not due for 5 weeks, but already she is starting to feel anxious. She has not written a paper for a long time.

Her teacher explained the writing process, and it made sense to her at the time. However, now that she has to begin writing her paper, she can remember only one point. She knows that she is supposed to be doing something called invention, but she does not remember what that is supposed to be.

## The Challenge

Writing a college-level essay can produce anxiety. Students may not have much experience writing. They often become stressed and cannot write at all. This writer's block is common in beginning composition classes.

## The Facts

Writing essays is not difficult if students remember the following five-step process. Each step of this process builds on an earlier step:

Step 1: Prewriting
The first stage of the process is called prewriting. In this stage, students create ideas to write about and figure out what they already know about the subject. In writing the standard five-paragraph essay, students discover what they know and organize their thoughts. In research papers, students usually do not know anything about the topic, and they do research to find information.

Step 2: Organizing
The next step in the process is for students to organize their thoughts. Most students create an outline to help them identify the three main points of their essay and create their thesis sentence. The thesis explains what the whole essay is about. In longer papers, students often use main points and sub-points in their outlines so that they can list every point they plan to write about in one place.

Step 3: Drafting

The outline helps students to know what they are writing about and the points that they want to make in their paper. Next, they must write the first draft. Many students feel a certain amount of anxiety about the drafting process because they misunderstand the purpose. In this step, students do not need to worry about grammar, punctuation or spelling.

Step 4: Revising

The revision or editing step allows students to go back over their rough draft and change it. They now need to look at spelling, grammar and punctuation. Students should read the paper one time for each item that they are looking for.

In this stage, students also may consider reorganizing their main points. Once the essay is written out, students may decide to switch points or delete a point entirely. Most students read their essay once just to check organization and structure.

Step 5: Proofreading

After students have checked for errors and looked at the organization one last time, they are ready to do a final proofreading. In this step, students should look for the smallest details, such as comma use, spaces between sentences and individual word choice.

## The Solutions

### Prewriting Techniques

The four most common prewriting techniques are listed below. Students who are having trouble deciding what to write about can follow the simple instructions for one or all of these techniques:

1. Brainstorming

Brainstorming is a technique that most students have used before. Students jot down a list of everything they can call to mind about a specific subject. Writing on a piece of paper is fine, but the best method is to use a larger space like a chalkboard.

Without thinking about the words, students should write down whatever ideas come to mind. No idea is bad. Keep writing ideas down until you feel as if you are devoid of ideas or the space you are writing on is full. Go through everything you have written and circle the ideas that appeal to you. From there, you can construct an outline to write your paper.

2. Free writing

Free writing is a little like brainstorming. Students should get paper and a pen and set a timer for 5 minutes. Once the time begins, they should put their pen down on the paper and write. They should write whatever comes into their heads. In fact, if they cannot think of anything, that is exactly what they should put on their papers: I do not know what to write. I do not know what to write....

3. Clustering/Mind mapping

Clustering, also called mind mapping or concept mapping, is a technique that works especially well for visual learners. Students should get a piece of paper or a larger surface, such as a chalk or dry erase board. First, they write a central idea and circle it. Then they write all the ideas that they can think of and draw lines to link them to the other circles. The lines indicate that the ideas are related.

For example, a student who has to write a narrative essay about her most frightening experience might write a mind map that included the following linked words:
Car accident–ran out of gas–gauge not working–cell phone dead–late at night.

4. Outline

Some students have very orderly minds. For them, the best prewriting technique is to create an outline. After the outline is written, students can go back and reorganize the main points they plan to use in the essay.

## Organizing Techniques

Students can organize their essays in a number of ways. Some of the most common methods are listed below:

- Time order

  One common method for organizing a paper is time order, also called chronological order. In this technique, writers organize their main points according to what step comes first in time. A paper organized in this way is sometimes called a process paper because the writer explains the process of how something works, and many processes need to work in time order.

- Least important to most important, or regular pyramid/Most important to least important, or inverted pyramid

  Some writers like to organize their papers based on the relative importance of their main points. For example, a writer may decide to start with the weakest example first and then work up to the strongest example. This technique allows writers to end with their strongest points in order to leave readers with a good impression of their arguments.

  Other writers like to use the inverted pyramid style, also called the newspaper style, to organize their papers. In this technique, the writer begins with the most important point in order to get the reader's attention and ends with the weakest argument or example.

- Narrative

  This is often the best way to organize a paper about an experience that the writer had, such as a first date. While this technique is similar to time order, the writer may begin the narrative at the end of the story and then explain what happened before that.

- Compare and contrast

  Writers frequently like to organize their papers in a compare-and-contrast style. In this technique, the writer chooses two ideas and compares them—that is, shows how they are alike—or contrasts them—shows how they are different.

- Description

  Writers who are good at using adjectives and adverbs often like to organize their essays using description. As the name implies, they describe a place, a person or an object using sensory details.

- Classification

  Another good way to organize an essay is by classifying ideas, objects or people into categories. For example, a writer may use this technique to describe the three types of people he has met in college: professors, serious students and future dropouts.

- How-to

  Writers can explain how to do something in their essays by using the how-to technique. This method uses description and time order to explain how to complete a process. For example, a student might write an essay about how to be a barista at a coffee shop. The three main points might be as follows:
  1. Take order from customer;
  2. translate order into barista-speak such as skinny cow no beard for skim milk no foam; and
  3. create the drink.

## The Resources

The following resources offer more information about writing techniques and seeing yourself as a writer:

*www.utexas.edu/student/utlc/lrnres/handouts/1318.html*

The Website from the University of Texas at Austin offers suggestions about building a positive image of yourself as a writer.

*http://leo.stcloudstate.edu/acadwrite/block.html*

This Website from the Literacy Education Online (LEO) center at St. Cloud State University in Minnesota offers assistance with overcoming writer's block.

# Using the Internet &
# Avoiding Plagiarism

A freshman in junior college is writing a research paper for her English class. She is halfway through her research when she realizes that she has 50 index cards full of information, but she cannot remember if the notes are direct quotations or her own paraphrase of the information.

The student understands a little about plagiarism because her teacher has talked about it many times. While she does not want to go back to every source and check her notes, she also does not want to be accused of plagiarism and possibly thrown out of school.

## The Challenge

Writing a research paper is difficult enough without having to deal with the issues surrounding plagiarism. However, these issues have arisen often in academic circles, and English professors in particular are clear about what will happen if a student cheats. The problem is that at least half of all plagiarism is unintentional. Students have taken notes in a disorganized fashion and cannot remember which ones are direct quotations and which are paraphrases.

For this reason, English teachers often hand out plagiarism worksheets to help their students understand the various types of intentional and unintentional plagiarism. In addition, a number of Websites have sprung up to help students understand how to reference everything from a conversation with an author to a fact found on an obscure Website.

## The Facts

Plagiarism is the act of representing someone else's ideas, words or images as your own. This can happen intentionally, as when a student knowingly copies a roommate's paper and hands it in as his or her own work. Plagiarism also can happen unintentionally, as when a student thinks that a note taken from a journal was a paraphrase of the original when it was in fact a direct quote.

Unfortunately, college officials are less interested in how plagiarism happens than they are in finding and punishing students who plagiarize. In general, faculty and administrators of colleges and universities will punish students who knew or should have known that what they were doing constituted plagiarism.

The following list describes the various types of plagiarism and how such incidents can occur:

- Intentional plagiarism
  - Borrowing, buying or stealing someone else's paper.
  - Hiring another student to write your paper.
  - Copying or paraphrasing from a source without citing it.

- Unintentional plagiarism
  - Paraphrasing the source too closely.
  - Building on someone else's idea without citing it.
  - Copying or paraphrasing from a source without citing it.

### No Need to Document

The following items do not require a citation in the student's paper:

Students' experiences, opinions, conclusions or experiments.
If students are writing about themselves including incidents from their lives, their opinions or conclusions they have drawn about a subject, they do not need a citation. It is obvious to the reader where the information comes from.

Common knowledge.
Students are not required to reference or cite anything that can be considered common knowledge. For academic purposes, common knowledge can include folklore, commonsense information or shared cultural data.

If students have questions about whether or not information is common knowledge, they can use the following methods to decide:
- If five other sources list the same information without referencing it, the information is probably common knowledge.
- If the information is something that students think their readers will know from other classes or real life, the information is almost certainly common knowledge.
- If students know that the information is easily available in general reference sources, the data is common knowledge.

## The Solutions

The most important factor in referencing information is to give credit where credit is due. In general, students should err on the side of over-citing their sources rather than risking plagiarism.

Every piece of information that is borrowed from another author or Website must be documented in the research paper. If students did not think of the ideas themselves, the information needs to be cited. The following types of information must be referenced in a research paper:

Direct quotes
> A direct quote occurs when a student uses the exact words of someone else. In a direct quote, students need to put quotation marks around the exact words attributed to the author or speaker and reference their name in the text of the paper. For example: Patrick Henry said "Give me liberty or give me death."

Paraphrases
> A paraphrase is a summary of the original quotation. To paraphrase correctly, students should not use any significant words from the original text. In addition, students still need to reference the author's name in the text of the paper. For example: According to Patrick Henry, dying was preferable if he could no longer live as a free man.

Ideas
> Even ideas that students did not think of themselves need to be referenced in their papers. While ideas themselves cannot be copyrighted, most English professors want their students to cite anything that they did not think of themselves. For example: Patrick Henry was a man who was prepared to die for his ideals.

Sayings, quotations or facts that are not common knowledge
> If information is not common knowledge, students need to cite that information and list the name of the author or the source in the text of the paper. However, if the information can be found easily in a common reference source, students do not need to cite it. For example, the following sentence is common knowledge and would not need a reference: Patrick Henry was an early leader of Colonial America.

## Sources That Must Be Documented

Some students believe that only printed books or articles need to be cited in a research paper. That is wrong. All sources of information that students did not create themselves must be referenced. The list below includes most of the sources of information that students will likely use for their research:

Printed materials
> Students need to reference all printed materials, including books, book chapters, magazines, journals, newspaper articles, diaries, letters, census documents and any other public documents.

Spoken or recorded
> Students also need to reference any spoken or recorded information,

such as class lectures, videos, movies, radio programs, speeches, conversations or interviews.

Electronic

In addition, students must reference any electronic materials that they access including Web pages, e-journals, e-zines, databases, newsgroup listings, bulletin board postings, podcasts, blogs and e-mail messages.

Images

Students need to cite any images that they discuss in their paper, including paintings, sculpture, illustrations, cartoons, charts, graphics, PowerPoint® presentations, Web graphics and tables.

## Tips for Avoiding Plagiarism

To avoid even the appearance of plagiarism, students need to make safety their first concern. The following tips can help:

Identify direct quotes when taking notes.

Students need to be careful when they are taking notes. They need to clearly label anything that is a direct quote. Some students do this by using quotation marks in their notes and on their notecards. Other students only use direct quotations in their notes, so they know that everything listed on a notecard is a direct quote. Another way to identify direct quotes in notes is to highlight them in a specific color.

List author, title and page number or URL for every source.

Anther way that students can protect themselves is to make sure that they list the author, title and page number or URL for every item written on a notecard, making it easy to verifly sources.

Keep a log.

Students who want to protect themselves from inadvertent plagiarism should keep a comprehensive research log. They should list every single item that they looked at during their research in the log and include the author, title, page number or URL. If the teacher questions a source, the student can produce the research log and avert any difficulties.

## The Resources

The following resources offer more information about avoiding plagiarism:

*http://college.hmco.com/english/plagiarism_prevention.html*

This Website from Houghton Mifflin's college division offers an online course to help students avoid plagiarism.

*www.umuc.edu/library/copy.html*

The Website from the University of Maryland University College explains copyright and fair use policies for college students and faculty.

# Using a Computer to Do Homework

A mother bought her daughter a computer to use in high school and learned that her daughter has been doing homework online. When she visited the Websites to make sure that they were appropriate, she was amazed at all the free information available.

Because the mother is a part-time college student, she looked at several online writing labs (OWLs) across the country and bookmarked the sites. The resources that her daughter was using were also helpful for college subjects.

## The Challenge

Today, students can get help with their homework from the Internet. Online tutoring sites and homework centers make it possible for students to get tutoring at all hours of the day and night. In addition, many low-cost or no-cost Websites offer expert analysis on science and math, historical information and writing advice.

With all of this information available all the time, students need to be able to distinguish the useful and reliable sights from those that are merely trying to sell something. Learning to question information from the Internet will help both high school and college students alike.

## The Facts

Students can get homework help from all over the globe on a wide variety of subjects—English, science, math, history, social studies and languages. In addition, many of these Websites offer help preparing for science fairs, research papers, speeches and class presentations. However, students must be able to verify the expert status of the authors and the truth of the information they encounter.

Because anyone can buy a domain name and create a Website, students need to be particularly concerned about the provenance of their information. Most Web pages need to have their authenticity verified.

In general, students can trust information from the following organizations, but all other Websites, particularly those selling goods or services, should be suspect:

- college and universities
- museums
- governmental agencies
- libraries

## The Solutions

Following are several reliable Websites organized by subject:

### Writing/English

*www.powa.org/*

This Website offers examples of many types of essays as well as worksheets about typical writing issues such as run-on sentences and punctuation errors. Some advertisements are included, but these are generally small.

*http://Webenglishteacher.com/*

Using this Website is like having an English teacher by your side. It includes links for writing, literature and poetry. Everything you need to know to do well in English is available here.

*www.askanexpert.com/*

Students who need an expert opinion to quote in their papers should visit this Website. Askanexpert.com offers links to a large number of experts in all fields. It is an excellent resource for science fair ideas, research and choosing a career.

### Math

*http://mathforum.org/library/drmath/drmath.high.html*

This Website from the Drexel School of Education at Drexel University is a great site for math questions. Ask Dr. Math has a full archive of information from fractions to calculus. Students can pose their own questions or view online explanations with sample problems.

*http://highschoolace.com/ace/ace.cfm*

This Website offers free information and homework help along with excellent college data. High school students who want to search for colleges while completing their math homework will have an easy time finding everything they need here.

*www.ies.co.jp/math/java/index.html*

This Website by International Education Software offers math applets and downloads that help students to better understand math concepts.

The multimedia approach is especially helpful for students who are kinesthetic learners. The interactive math programs offer insight into algebra, geometry and trigonometry.

## History

*www.thehistorynet.com/index.html*

This Website from the Weider History Group offers quizzes and an extensive archive of articles about historical events. The site also has a section entitled *Today in History* that can help students complete history homework or find appropriate paper topics. Much of the information is interesting as well as useful.

*www.sparknotes.com/*

This Website by Barnes & Noble® includes many homework resources as well as many cultural and entertainment pages for after the homework is completed. While it is largely a commercial site, students still can get their questions answered by experts, and it offers a variety of free online resources and low-cost .pdf documents.

## Science

*www.sciam.com/askexpert_directory.cfm*

This Web page from Scientific American magazine offers interesting questions and answers in every field of science. Students can pose their own questions or read answers to questions already posted there.

*www.exploratorium.edu/*

This Website from the Exploratorium Museum offers fascinating information about the synthesis of science, art and human perception. It features excellent images and is a good site to use for ideas on your next science project or art assignment.

*www.factmonster.com/*

Fact Monster from Infoplease.com has information about everything students will need to do their homework. When the homework is done, the Website also has interesting pages to look at and things to do. The graphics are intense, and the advertising is low-key.

## Reference/Research

*www.ala.org/ala/aasl/schlibrariesandyou/k12students/k12students.htm*

This Website from the American Library Association offers information about how to do research. The special section for students includes how to cite references and where to find good research.

*www.infoplease.com/*

This Website from Infoplease.com, the people who also offer Fact

Monster, lists all the online reference tools that students need to complete homework or write an essay.

*www.bartleby.com/*

The ultimate free reference center, Bartleby.com offers Bartlett's Familiar Quotations and a number of literary works that are out of copyright. For information, definitions and quotations, this Website is suitable for students and professionals alike.

## Online Tutoring

*http://homeworkhelp.tutor.com/*

Students who need live homework help also can go to this Website to get assistance 24 hours a day 7 days a week. The Website offers a free day pass for students to give the service a try and also works with businesses to offer expert advice to clients and employees.

## The Resources

The following Websites offer more information about using your computer to do homework:

*www.ipl.org/div/aplus/links.htm#writing*

This Website from the Internet Public Library offers a cornucopia of OWLs to help students with writing.

*http://essayinfo.com/*

This Website from the Essay Writing Center offers examples of every type of essay and many style guides.

# ACT, SAT & High School Test Preparation Classes, Books & Internet Courses

A mother has three children, the oldest of whom is a daughter in high school. Although she is only a sophomore, the daughter already is thinking about college. All of her friends are planning their study courses for the Scholastic Assessment Tests (SAT) or American College Test (ACT). One of them is going to a camp that promises to help students earn 100 extra points or more on the SAT®. Another is going to a well-known education company for private tutoring. The daughter wants to know what she should do to improve her test-taking abilities.

Because the mother did not have to take either test, she does not know what to tell her daughter. She wants to help her succeed on the tests, but she does not have money to send her to a private tutor or a summer camp.

## The Challenge

In order to gain admission to the nation's top colleges and universities, many students take extra study courses, use online instruction or private tutors and attend summer camps to improve their scores on the SAT and ACT. Most parents believe that improving their children's scores on these important tests will guarantee them admission. While many admission committees do require one of these tests, most colleges and universities also look at students' academic record in high school, their volunteer activities and their involvement in extracurricular programs.

While some studies have shown that private tutoring and personal coaching classes can improve students' scores on these tests, they can cost $700 or more. Students of moderate means often opt for the test books put out by the companies that create the tests and online courses.

## The Facts

Good coaching can help students improve their scores on the ACT and SAT, which can help them get accepted at the better colleges and universities. It has been theorized that graduating from a well-regarded college can give students an edge in their first job hunt, their future careers and even their overall success in life. However, that is just a theory. Students determine their own careers and success, but those who are able to pay for private tutoring do have an easier time doing well on these tests.

## The Solutions

### SAT and ACT Online

The best place to begin a search for preparation materials is the official Websites of the ACT and SAT:

*www.collegeboard.com/student/testing/sat/prep_one/prep_one.html*

The official SAT Website from the College Board includes an official online course, the official study guide, a free SAT practice test and various practice questions. Students are given a discount for buying both the online course and the study guide.

*www.actstudent.org/testprep/*

The official ACT Website offers many of the same options as the SAT site. They have an online course, a study guide and sample tests that students can purchase. In addition, the ACT site offers students an 80-page guide for study at no charge along with sample tests, test tips and descriptions of the test itself.

*www.actstudent.org/onlineprep/index.html*

The Act Online Prep course costs $20 for a 1-year subscription. It includes practice tests, practice essays, content review and a diagnostic test complete with a personalized study plan. The advantage and disadvantage of this course is the same—students need to be self-motivated.

### Tutoring Services

Many students opt for personal coaching services. These educational courses range from actual class presentations with 30 or more other students to one-on-one tutoring to help with specific test-taking issues.

Two of the biggest companies in this venue are The Princeton Review and Kaplan.

*www.princetonreview.com*

The Princeton Review offers both SAT and ACT test prep services as well as individual tutors. Their classroom courses promise no more than 12 students per class. They also offer online courses with lessons and drills. For no charge, they offer students an online practice test, a word of the day Website and reports from their experts on the latest versions of the ACT and SAT.

Their in-person classes range from $700 to $900, depending on how much help the student needs. They also offer a $900 class for sophomores to help them take the test in their junior or senior years.

Their online courses range from $80 to $600 and include online modules, drills and practice tests. For $2,000, students can get the online course plus 18 hours of personal tutoring online.

*www.kaptest.com*

Kaplan Test Prep and Admissions offers preparation for both tests, including in-person classes, online classes and private tutoring. Their Website contains test-taking tips and an *SAT QuizBank* free of charge.

Their in-person classes offer personal attention, realistic practice and special tips to help students score more points. The cost is $700 for the in-class course, and the online course is priced at $300.

## Coaching Camps

There are a number of coaching camps available for high school students. Some offer specific ACT/SAT preparation for juniors and seniors as well as academic boot camp for younger students.

*www.brightonedge.org*

Students spend 10 days at either UCLA or Tufts University. The program is open to sophomores, juniors and seniors. Students learn test-taking strategies and attend guest lectures. The cost is $2,500 for students who will live on campus and $1,200 for day-students and includes meals, trips and guest speakers.

*www.supercamp.com*

SuperCamp! offers academic programs to students from fourth to 12th grades, including a new leadership forum for students who have already completed at least one previous SuperCamp! The program also offers a college forum for students 18 to 24 years old that covers a variety of study skills including motivation, memory techniques, and note taking and reading skills. The fees range form $1,800 for a 7-day camp for fourth- and fifth-graders to $2,600 for a 10-day experience at Stanford University.

## Books for SAT/ACT Prep

There are also a number of books for test preparation. The following is a list of the most popular ones, according to Amazon.com®. The last one is a book written by students who scored well on the SAT and share their experience and advice.

- *Cracking the ACT, 2005 Edition* from the Princeton Review
- *Barron's How to Prepare for the ACT* by George Ehrenhaft, et al.
- *Cracking the new SAT, 2006 Edition* from the Princeton Review
- *Up Your Score: The Underground Guide to the SAT: Revised for 2005-2006* by Larry Berger, et al.

### Books for General Testing and Test Anxiety

The following books are useful for students who want to know more about test-taking and study strategies and avoiding test stress:

- *What Smart Students Know* by Adam Robinson
- *Test Taking Strategies and Study Skills for the Utterly Confused* by Laurie Rozakis
- *How to Do Your Best on Tests (School Survival Guide)* by Sara Dulaney Gilbert
- *Study Smarter, Not Harder* by Kevin Paul
- *No More Test Anxiety: Effective Steps for Taking Tests and Achieving Better Grades* by Ed Newman

## The Resources

The following Websites, books and other resources offer more information about FREE SAT resources:

*www.vocabulary.com*

This Website has advertising on it, but it offers excellent online classes that will help students build their vocabularies.

*www.collegeboard.com/apps/qotd/question*

This Website from the College Board, the people who create the SAT, offers a free SAT question of the day.

*www.number2.com*

This Website offers free ACT and SAT online instruction. The site includes some advertising, but their purpose is to offer excellent coaching so that all students can succeed on these tests.

*www.essayedge.com/college/admissions/satcourse*

This Website offers free SAT course information, practice questions and vocabulary instruction. It includes advertising, and their core service is editing students' papers, including essays written for college applications.

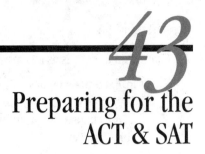

# Preparing for the ACT & SAT

## The Challenge

Most college students take either the SAT or the ACT before they enter college. These tests are usually a requirement to apply. In fact, some students and their parents are so intent on getting into elite colleges that they pay to take preparation classes that promise to help students increase their scores.

Other students buy books that promise to give secret tips for succeeding on these tests, and there are now many Websites that help students practice their test-taking skills. While the SAT and ACT are important to college-bound students, they are just standardized tests, and students can use the same skills that they practiced in high school to help them succeed.

## The Facts

### ACT

The ACT consists of the following four sections:

- The English section is 75 questions timed over 45 minutes. This part of the assessment is supposed to test standard written English and rhetorical skills learned in high school.
- The math section is 60 questions timed over 60 minutes. This part of the assessment is supposed to test basic math skills acquired up to the beginning of the senior year in high school.
- The reading section is 40 questions timed over 35 minutes. This part of the assessment is supposed to test reading comprehension.
- The science section is also 40 questions timed over 35 minutes. This part of the assessment is supposed to test interpretation, analysis, evaluation, reasoning and problem-solving skills in the natural sciences.

Students also can take an optional writing test on the ACT. This test is timed for 30 minutes and is supposed to test skills taught in high school English classes as well as beginning composition classes in college.

Scoring on the ACT is as follows:

- ACT scoring includes only the number of questions you answered correctly. There is no penalty for wrong answers. For this reason, most experts advise students to guess on the ACT if they have even a vague idea of the correct answer.

## SAT

The SAT is created by the College Board. The test has the following eight sections:

There are three verbal reasoning sections. Two of these sections cover sentence completions, analogies and critical reading. One covers only critical reading.

- Section 1–30 or 31 questions timed over 30 minutes
- Section 2–35 or 36 questions timed over 30 minutes
- Section 3–critical reading only–12 or 13 questions timed over 15 minutes

There are three math reasoning sections.

- Section 1–multiple-choice–25 questions timed over 30 minutes
- Section 2–quantitative comparisons/grid-ins–25 questions timed over 30 minutes
- Section 3–multiple choice–10 questions timed over 15 minutes

There are two writing sections:

- Section 1–direct writing–essay written over 25 minutes
- Section 2–multiple choice–timed over 35 minutes.

The writing section was added in 2005. In 2006, the multiple-choice questions in the writing section may be divided into two parts.

The order of the sections varies, but each section except critical reading starts with easy questions and ends with difficult questions. All questions are worth one point.

Scoring on the SAT is as follows:

- Students are awarded one point for correct answers. They are awarded zero points for unanswered questions. In addition, .25 points is subtracted from their scores for incorrect answers. Even with the 0.25-point deduction for wrong answers, experts advise students to guess an answer if they can eliminate at least one of the distracters.

### A Word about Vocabulary on the ACT and SAT

Both the SAT and the ACT test your knowledge of vocabulary words. Students can increase their scores by learning more words. The following are several ways to do this:

- buying a vocabulary book especially designed for these assessments

- using flashcards
- visiting Websites that have vocabulary-building programs such as *www.dictionary.com*, *www.freevocabulary.com* and *www.act-sat-prep.com*

### Preparing for Test Day

Students who want to be successful on the ACT or SAT need to do more than study, take practice tests and improve their vocabularies. They also need to take care of themselves and rest. The following tips can help students improve their test scores:

Sleep well
> For the few days before the test, students should get 8 to 9 hours of sleep every night. Students who suffer from test anxiety, also called test stress, need to exercise each day, including test day, to help themselves relax.

Eat breakfast
> Studies have shown that students who eat breakfast do better on cognition and comprehension tests than those who do not.

Bring acceptable identification and the admission ticket
> Each test has a specific list of identification that will be accepted at the door. Students also need to bring the admission ticket that each testing agency sends out and a picture I.D.

Bring three No. 2 pencils
> Mechanical pencils and pens are not allowed on these tests. Bring extra just in case one breaks.

Calculator with fresh batteries, if allowed
> If you are allowed to use a calculator for your test, remember to bring fresh batteries. The rules about calculators are included with the information from each testing center.

Healthy snacks
> A break is scheduled for the middle of the testing period in most testing centers.

Arrive early
> Make sure that you are at the testing center no later than 15 minutes before the test begins. Testing starts at 8 a.m. sharp, and testing centers will not let students in after the start time.

## The Solutions

### General Tips—ACT
Pace yourself
> Make sure that you watch the clock during each section. Do not spend too much time on any one question.

Answer easy questions first

Unlike the SAT, the questions in the ACT are not organized from easy to difficult. However, they do include easy, intermediate and difficult questions, and all of them are worth the same number of points. Therefore, answer all the easy questions first and then go back and answer the others.

Read questions carefully

Standardized tests are notorious for having tricky instructions. Read every detail carefully and make sure that you know exactly what you are being asked to do.

Answer all questions

Because the ACT has no penalty for guessing, answer every question.

## General Tips—SAT

Easy first

The SAT starts with the easy questions and ends with the difficult ones. Each question is worth the same number of points. For this reason, answer all the easy questions first.

Guessing is okay most of the time

Experts advise that students guess if they can recognize that at least one of the distracters is wrong. If you can eliminate just one of them, you can look at the others and guess with an excellent chance of being correct.

Not necessary to answer every question to get a good score

According to the experts, students should skip any questions that make no sense to them or that they know nothing about. Unanswered questions are counted as zero.

Use test booklet to keep track of questions answered

You can use the test booklet itself to keep track of the questions that you answered. You may want to keep track so that you can check the answer sheet to make sure that you marked the correct boxes.

Pace yourself

Keep an eye on the clock so that you not spend too much time on any one question. Remember, all the questions are worth one point.

## The Resources

The following Website offers more information about preparing for the ACT or SAT:

*www.Internet4classrooms.com/act_sat.htm*

This Website offers an excellent annotated list of online resources for students taking either the ACT or SAT. It offers a variety of free test tips, study guides and information about which sites offer the best information. However, there are more SAT sites listed than ACT sites.

# Do Tutoring Centers Really Work?

A mother wants to get some individualized help for her oldest daughter, who is already thinking about taking the ACT even though she is only a sophomore. Meanwhile, her son is having problems with English class. He is in the sixth grade and does not like to write.

She would like to get her son a personal tutor, but they are quite expensive. She is thinking about investigating a well-known tutoring center such as Sylvan or Kaplan, but those also may not be within her budget. She would be willing to spend the money if she could be sure that her children would benefit from it.

## The Challenge

Parents spend thousands of dollars each year on tutors, testing centers and tutoring centers in an attempt to help their children succeed at school. Some parents question the efficacy of tutoring centers, especially those with a recognizable name. They wonder what makes these centers work and if they are worth the price, especially if their children have learning disabilities.

## The Facts

The truth is that learning centers such as Kaplan and Sylvan actually do help children learn and succeed in school. However, several caveats are discussed below.

The centers give diagnostic tests and offer individualized programs to suit each child's learning style and skill set. For most children, this one-on-one teaching helps. They can answer questions without feeling foolish, and the centers make learning fun by offering prizes and incentives. In addition, the individualized instruction and copious amounts of practice help these students feel more confident in their abilities. This newfound confidence helps them improve their test scores.

The centers also can help parents feel confident that their children will go on to college. Many high school tests require students to pass before they can graduate, and parents can pay to have them tutored before these tests. In fact, they can have their children tutored for any standardized test. Since the scores of these tests impact the direction their children will take as they move through the school system, many parents want to provide their children with as much of an edge as possible.

In addition, Kaplan also offers complete study packages for both the SAT and ACT, including classes, online tutorials and one-on-one tutors that can help students get admitted to elite colleges and universities.

### Steps to Take Before Hiring a Tutor

Experts advise parents to do some investigation before sending their children to tutoring or learning centers. Depending on the age of the child and the particular learning issue, some problems can be worked out at school with the teacher.

Step 1: Talk to the teacher.

If a child is having trouble in school, parents need to talk to the teacher first. Teachers usually have experience with how students learn, and they spend time with your child every day. Find out if the teacher thinks your child needs to get a tutor or just pay more attention in class. If the teacher thinks that your child needs to be tested for a learning disability, do so.

Step 2: Check vision and hearing.

After talking to the teacher, consider having your child tested for visual or hearing problems. Students cannot do well in school if they cannot see the board or hear the teacher's directions. Often a hearing or sight problem is all that is the matter.

Step 3: Observe social maturity.

Does your child get along well with other students? Is he or she very insecure about peer pressure? Some children may not do as well in school because they are more interested in social activities than in academics. In addition, parents should make sure that their children are not promoted to the next grade unless they have learned the basics. If children do not learn the building blocks of reading and math in grade school, they can spend the rest of their academic careers trying to catch up.

Step 4: Look at time management and organizational skills.

As children mature, their classes get more difficult. By sixth grade, many children are going to a different class for each subject. Middle school or junior high school is a time when students may do poorly because they do not understand how to organize their study materials or manage their time.

Before sending sixth- to eighth-grade students to a tutoring center, make sure that they are writing down their homework assignments and taking notes in class. Also, monitor the time they spend watching television, playing video games and talking to their friends.

Step 5: Test for learning disabilities.

If parents have tried all four previous steps, the final step before tutoring is to have your child tested. Schools are required to test students who may have a learning disability at no charge to the parent. This is at the discretion of the child's teacher or the school administration. Talk to the school principal.

Step 6: Investigate private tutor.

You are now faced with some choices. Do you hire a private tutor to come to your house, take your child to a tutoring center or become the tutor yourself? If your child does have a learning disability, you can get him or her special help at school from a special education teacher or a resource specialist.

If you decide to hire a private tutor, read the chapter in this book about how to hire one. The two most important factors are the person's education and how the person relates to your child. If possible, try to find a tutor who has taught public school. In addition, make sure that your child has a good relationship with this person.

Children with learning disabilities also can benefit from a private tutor. The tutor will need specific credentials for teaching these students.

Step 7: Investigate tutoring center.

If your children work better in a group setting, you may consider enrolling them in a tutoring center. Most centers have students work in small groups with a tutor. They are tested and their practice is determined by their skills and abilities. In addition, many tutoring centers also offer one-on-one tutoring.

Step 8: Investigate parental tutoring.

Some parents want to undertake the tutoring responsibilities themselves. This can be a problem. Parents may have difficulty getting their children to listen to them. In addition, tutoring your own children can be time-consuming and frustrating. Parents who have degrees in education may want to try it, but other parents may not have the time, expertise or stamina.

## The Solutions

### What Every Parent Should Know about Tutoring Centers

Tutoring centers seldom mention the things that they will not or cannot do for your children. For this reason, parents who are considering a tutoring center should read the following information:

- Available scholarships

  Tutoring centers do not advertise it, but most of them offer discounts and scholarships if parents ask about them. If they do not offer scholarships, they may offer volume discounts to parents who pay in advance for future tutoring sessions.

- No required educational standards

  Public and even private schools must adhere to educational standards from the federal and state governments. Tutoring centers are not held to any such standards.

- Quality can vary

  Parents need to ask about the qualifications of the tutors at each center. Be specific. Some franchises hire only certified public school teachers, while others do not require tutors to have a teaching background at all.

- Fees for testing

  Some tutoring centers charge extra fees to test your children. Before you agree to such tests, check to make sure that your child's school has not administered a similar test already. Ask if a school test can be substituted in place of the center-sponsored test.

- Different tutors

  Most tutoring centers do not tell parents that their children may see a different tutor at every session. If your child needs one-on-one tutoring, ask the center director if you can schedule time with a specific tutor. The relationship between your child and the tutor is important. If your child has a good experience, he or she will learn faster.

## The Resources

The following resources offer more information about tutoring centers:

*www.sylvan.com*

This Website for Sylvan explains their tutoring strategies and their prices.

*www.kaptest.com*

This Website from Kaplan explains their guarantee, their policies and their prices.

*www.huntingtonlearning.com/*

This Website from Huntington explains their tutors, their teaching process and their prices.

# Organizing Research

A college freshman is working on a research paper for her English class. She has done the research, but she does not know how to organize her notecards or proceed to the next step.

Her teacher has talked about writing an outline and creating a thesis statement, but the student does not understand how to translate the hundreds of notecards in front of her into either of these.

She wishes that she make all of this happen instantly. She does not mind writing the research paper, but she would like to know how all the parts fit together.

## The Challenge

To many students, the various tasks involved with writing a research paper can seem like parts of wildly dissimilar projects. Finding research materials takes one set of skills, while organizing those materials into a coherent thesis statement and outline requires an entirely different set.

Writing this kind of paper is one of the most difficult kinds of assignments in college. Students who excel in this endeavor have learned how to break the project into small, workable tasks so that they can accomplish each one without being overwhelmed by the impending deadline.

The research paper has three distinct stages. The first stage involves choosing a topic, doing research on that topic and taking notes. The second involves organizing the research notes, either notecards or electronic files, into a workable thesis statement and outline for the paper. This stage also requires students to keep track of their sources and keep a log of each item they look at while researching their papers, which will prevent them from inadvertently committing plagiarism. The third stage requires students to use everything they have learned about writing an essay to take the paper from outline to final draft.

## The Facts

Organizing the notes is only one of three steps in the process of organizing the research. The other two steps are organizing your thesis statement and organizing your outline. The following two sections offer tips to help students complete both tasks.

## Organizing Thesis Statement

The first step is to stretch your research topic into a full-fledged thesis statement. The process is not difficult, but it can be tricky for students doing it for the first time. For example, a research topic such as images of women in Jane Austen's *Pride and Prejudice* would be difficult to write about because there is no argument. A good thesis statement needs an arguable point–a point that not everyone would agree with and a point that you can prove with your research.

A better thesis statement could be dividing the women in Austen's work into three types as follows: the foolish children–Elizabeth Bennett's mother and the sister who runs away with Wickham; women who are agreeable, pliant and hide their brains–Elizabeth Bennett's oldest sister and her friend who gets married off to the vicar; and women who are as smart as men and not afraid to show it–Elizabeth Bennett herself and maybe Lady Catherine de Bourg. This classification scheme is arguable by anyone who has read the book. Even the professor may not agree with the women chosen for each category.

Other traits of a good thesis statement are listed below:

A good thesis causes much information to be unimportant.
>Once the point is clear about the three divisions of women in *Pride and Prejudice*, readers do not need much more information because they understand what the paper will be about. If students have to explain their thesis statement, it is not clear enough.

A good thesis makes a point that you alone can discuss.
>Obviously, the sample thesis only makes sense to the person who created the divisions. Other writers might divide the women into different groups or disagree with which characters fall into which categories. Still others may have tried to categorize the men.

A good thesis gives your paper direction and helps build your argument.
>After reading the thesis statement above, the organization of the paper is clear. The writer needs to create three sections, one about each type of woman supported by examples from the text and scholars that prove the arguable point.

A good thesis frequently says something a little weird.
>Dividing characters into categories is a little strange. A good thesis needs to be original and creative. A commonplace statement does not need to be proved.

A good thesis fits the following Fabulous Thesis Holder (FTH) sentence written by

Erik Simpson of Grinnell College: By looking at _____, we can see _____, which most readers do not see; this is important because _____.

The thesis statement above fits into the FTH model: By looking at the women in *Pride and Prejudice*, we can see that Austen divides them into three types; this fact is important because Austen was making a statement about the society of her time.

### Organizing Outline

Once students have created a good thesis, they can put together an outline fairly quickly. Unless your teacher requires it, the outline does not need to be formal. It is just a way to organize your thoughts before you write the paper. The following tips will help you:

- •Thesis

  The thesis is the first step in creating an outline. The next steps all stem from it.
- • Main points

  What are you main points? Limit them to no more than five. Two to three main points are suitable for a 10- to 15-page paper. Try to think like your reader. What does your reader need to know, and when does the reader need to know it? Put the points in order and end with your strongest one.
- • Supporting points

  List your supporting points or the examples that prove each of your main points. List these as sub-points in your outline.
- • Research

  Number your notecards or electronic list to correspond with the outline. This way you will know which piece of research goes with which point. This final organization will make writing your paper much easier.

## The Solutions

Before students can move forward with their thesis statement or outline, they need to make sure that all of their research notes are organized correctly. Disorganized notes can result in a disorganized paper. Students can keep their research paper on track by following the tips below:

### Notecards

The traditional method for organizing research is using notecards, also called index cards. Students write on the cards and organize them according to the information on each one. Students also can use a three-ring binder with pocket dividers. Each section in the binder can correspond to a resource you looked at or a point you plan to make in the paper. The advantage of these methods is that notecards and binders are portable and inexpensive.

### Electronic Labels

Students with easy access to computers can set up electronic labels in their word processing software and use them as bibliography and notecards. Each label can include all the information on the book. The advantage is that electronic versions can be manipulated easily to create an almost perfect bibliography from scratch.

### Electronic Bookmarks

Students also can create a word processing document and use the electronic bookmark function to bookmark sections in their notes. All the notes for a particular subject can be typed into one document with all of the bibliographical information bookmarked. The advantage of this method is having all the information in one place.

### PowerPoint® Notes

Students who are familiar with PowerPoint can create a slide show for each research topic for their paper. They can include appropriate information on each card. Each subject could be a presentation that includes the notes and bibliography cards.

## The Resources

The following Websites, books and other resources offer more information about organizing research:

*www.utm.utoronto.ca/~dwhite/papers.htm*

This Website from the University of Toronto has everything you ever wanted to know about the entire research process, including organizing your research.

*www.bc.edu/libraries/services/ref-instruc/s-reach6*

This Website from Boston University explains research in the electronic age, including step-by-step explanations of how to organize your research.

*www.crlsresearchguide.org/14_Making_An_Outline.asp*

Organizing research is all about the search for a paper outline. This Website from Cambridge Rindge and Latin School is an excellent source of information.

*www.studygs.net/wrtstr5.htm*

Students who need to organize their notecards can use the simple guide on this Website from Study Guides and Strategies, which includes many other good paper-writing strategies as well.

*www.math.grinnell.edu/~simpsone/Teaching/fiveways.html*

This article from Erik Simpson, a literature professor at Grinnell College, answers all the important questions about what a good thesis should include.

# Using a Computer to Do Internet Research

A college student is using the Internet to find information for a research project. His teacher said that the research should not take more than an hour with a fast connection. So far the student has been searching for 3 hours and has not found everything he is looking for

The project is for his biology class. He is trying to find information about marine mammals such as dolphins and whales. His initial search returned over 10,000 sites. He has not even gotten halfway through the list, and he still does not have enough information to complete the project.

The student knows that the Internet is supposed to be a fast and easy way to find information, but he has had little success.

## The Challenge

Most college students already have a great deal of experience using the Web. They have e-mailed friends, used instant messaging and probably shopped for music, ring tones or books online. However, these experiences do not mean that students know how to find credible research on the Internet.

Good research is available, but students need to evaluate sites to determine whether or not they are useful for college research. This skill is not difficult to develop. Students need to begin with a basic distrust of anything they read on the Web. Anyone with a computer can build a Website claiming to be an expert on a subject, regardless of their actual qualifications.

## The Facts

Before students begin conducting research on the Internet, they need to understand how to evaluate each Website's value for their project. The following list includes tips to help students identify reliable sources:

### Content

What content is included on the Website? Students can read introductions, home pages and the table of contents to find out what each site covers.

### Audience

Who is the intended audience for the Website? Does it seem aimed at college-level students or scholars? What specific information leads you to believe this? Websites for consumers usually include only generalities. They may be useful for an overview of a topic, but they will not provide enough detail for a college project.

### Source

What was the Website designed to do? Who is the author? Is the site designed to sell the author's book, service or product? This may make the content suspect. Does the author list other sites for reference or as resources? These may prove useful.

Does the author provide an annotated bibliography of books, articles or other Websites? This information may provide you with other sources.

Is the site created or hosted by a college or university? These sites are often excellent sources for valid research and contain links to other good sites. Other reliable sources are sites sponsored by governmental agencies, not-for-profit organizations and foundations.

### Authority

What is the author's authority? Is he or she a professor at a college? Is this person an avowed expert? Who says that this person is an expert? Is this source credible? Does the author have an advanced degree such as a doctorate or a medical degree? What are the author's credentials? Has the author written books on the subject? How were these books received in the press?

### Bias

Does the author or the Website seem biased in favor of one opinion over another? Most Websites, books and articles are in fact biased, and this is not always a bad thing. Students need to figure out the bias of the author in order to evaluate whether the source will be useful for the research project. Good authors typically reveal their bias in the first page or two of their work.

### Date

How old is the content? Does it list a date or a copyright date? Information without a date can be suspect. Scientists and others are learning new information every day. Websites that are even 5 years old can contain inaccurate information. Before you quote from a Website or reference the content, verify the information at several other sites.

## The Solutions

### Efficient Internet Research

Many students have difficulty researching on the Internet because they get sidetracked. Remind yourself over and over again exactly what you are searching for. You can find information about any topic on the Internet, but you do not have time to look at everything. The rules below will help you use your research time wisely:

15 minute rule

Do not spend too much time at one Website. If you do not find any useful information in 10 to 15 minutes, abandon the site and move on to the next one.

One or two sites rule

Do not do all of your research on one or two Websites. Teachers frown at research formed by only a few opinions. If you find a rich site, bookmark it and move on. You can always go back and look at it later.

Bookmark and organization rule

Bookmark every site that you look at. You can create separate bookmark files for those sites that seem useful and those that do not. You also can create a folder for Websites you plan to use in your paper and those that you do not plan to use. Bookmarking these sites will make it easier for you to go back and find a specific Web page that you forgot to list.

Overview then print rule

Do not waste paper by printing out all the information from every Web page. Spend a few minutes looking around. If the Website seems useful for your purposes, print a few pages that you think will help. Make sure that the URL appears on the bottom of the pages. If it is not, make sure to bookmark the site or write the URL on the top of the printout.

## Search Engines

Students probably already know a number of excellent search engines. While any search engine will do, some of them may be better for helping students find academic journals and college libraries. Regardless of which one you use, you need to create a search that gives you enough Websites to visit but not so many that you will spend days going through them. Follow the tips below to create and narrow your search parameters:

## Creating a Search

Choosing words

Choose words that will help you find information on your topic. For example, if you are researching killer whales, you could type the word orca into the search engine. However, that may give you hundreds of Websites, and you will need to narrow your search.

Many search engines do not recognize capitalization. Check the search information for each search engine to see if they include or exclude capital letters.

Common words

> Most search engines do not want you to use common words such as of, in, a, etc. Some automatically delete these terms.

Phrases

> If common words are necessary to your topic, you can search for exact words by putting the word or phrase in quotation marks. For example, a search for information about the play *The Unbearable Lightness of Being* might include the following: unbearable lightness of being + reviews. This would return Websites that include reviews for the play.

Excluding items

> Students also can remove items such as words that have more than one meaning from their search using a minus sign. For example, the following search string would remove all the reviews from a search about the play: unbearable lightness of being - reviews + commentary.

## The Resources

The following resources offer more information about finding or evaluating Internet research:

*www.google.com/help/refinesearch.html*

> Students who need to narrow their search should consider reading the Google advanced search page at the URL above. If you know the basics, you need to know the advanced features of Google in order to make your Internet research as fast and efficient as possible.

*www.lib.purdue.edu/ugrl/staff/sharkey/interneteval/docs/worksheet3.pdf*

> This Website from Purdue University offers a .pdf worksheet to help students evaluate each Website they encounter.

*www.quick.org.uk/menu.htm*

> This Website explains how to determine if a Website is a good source for your research paper.

*www.uwec.edu/library/Guides/tencs.html*

> This Website from the University of Wisconsin-Eau Claire offers an in-depth explanation of how to evaluate a Website for college-level research papers.

*http://library.usm.maine.edu/research/researchguides/webevaluating.html*

> This Website from the University of Maine offers a concise explanation of evaluating Websites.

# Using Your Research &
# Writing to
# Prove Your Thesis

A college-bound junior is trying to pull together all of her information, her outline and her thesis sentence so she can write the rough draft of her term paper. However, she does not know how to use her research to prove her point.

The student has written papers before, but they were just five-paragraph essays. Her research paper is supposed to be 10 to 15 pages. While she understands the basic idea and has a good thesis and outline, she does not know where to go from there. She understands the overall idea, but she does not know how to get started.

## The Challenge

Even students who understand the big picture of writing a research paper can be bogged down when asked to explain the specifics. In particular, sitting down to write the rough draft can be difficult. Students with a good thesis and outline have an advantage, but they still need to understand how to take that next step. Writing a paragraph in a research paper is unlike any other kind of essay writing.

In a research paper, students need to prove their point with research–that is, with things that other people have said rather than their own opinions. This can be troublesome. Students also must figure out the appropriate tone, audience and point of view to maintain in a formal paper.

## The Facts

One important consideration when writing a research paper is audience, the person or persons you are writing for. Because he or she assigned the work, your teacher or teaching assistant will be your reader and therefore your audience.

You need to organize your essay so that it will make the most sense to your audience. Many college writers do not know how much detail to include. They know that their teacher or TA knows more than they do about the subject, but the main purpose of the research project is to show their own knowledge and persuasion/argumentation skills.

Before students write the first sentence of their rough draft, they need to consider their audience and answer the following questions:

- Who is my audience for this paper?
- Do I have more than one audience? Who are they?
- What does each audience want or need?
- What is most important to each audience?
- What does each audience not care about?
- Can you organize your essay so that it will be easier for each audience to understand? How?
- What impression do you want to make on each audience? What do you want them to think about you and your argument?

## The Solutions

### Essay as Argument

Many writing experts describe the research paper as a type of argument. While students will use their skills of persuasion and description in this paper, they will mainly be putting forth an argument and then proving their point. The framework for the argument is the thesis sentence, which lists the main points of the argument and provides the student's point of view for the essay.

### Using PEE Style

PEE is an acronym that stands for Points, Evidence and Explanation. This writing system can help students understand how to add their research to the essay. The technique works as follows:

Point

Make a point. For most students, this will be the topic sentence of the paragraph. This topic sentence also needs to be directly related to the thesis statement. Every paragraph in the paper needs to develop the thesis or argument a little more.

Evidence

Include a supporting quotation from a secondary source such as a Website, an article or book by a scholar in the field or from the primary text. This supporting quote must relate directly to your topic sentence and amplify it. Use only the section of the quotation that illustrates your point. Long, boring quotations will not help your argument.

Explanation

The rest of your paragraph needs to explain the quote and bolster your argument. This portion of the paragraph should take up the most space because you need to make sure that your audience understands what the quote means, how it proves the point you made and how it is related to the overall thesis for the paper.

## Parts of the Research Paper Essay

As noted before, writing a research paper includes a number of tasks that lead up to the creation of a longer essay. The final step in this process is drafting and editing the paper itself. All the research, planning and thinking that the student has done culminate in this step. The five-paragraph essay style is expanded for the research paper. Students should follow the tips below to write clear and effective sentences for each section of their paper:

Introduction

As with the five-paragraph essay, the introduction for your research paper will alert the reader to the themes and topics you will discuss in the paper. Think of this paragraph or series of paragraphs as a pyramid on its apex. Start with general language and ideas. Intensify your point until the last thing you write is the thesis sentence.

Some students begin by discussing the historical period they are writing about. For example, if you were writing your paper about science, you might detail what common people thought about science, the state of scientific methods during this time period and what leading scientific leaders of the time were studying.

Body Paragraphs

All of the paragraphs in the middle of your paper–between the introduction and the conclusion–are called the body paragraphs. You can have as few as three body paragraphs or as many as 50 or 60. Each body paragraph should help you build your argument with more and more examples that prove your point.

Think of a discussion between two men about the best automobile on the market. One talks about the reasonable price of his car. The other talks about the enhanced performance of his car, discusses the gas mileage and ends by giving the price he paid.

The second man is building an argument with proof. He knows that his audience, the other man, is most interested in the price of the car, so he intentionally saves that information for the end. In addition, his second point is about how much money he saves on gas because of the car's fuel economy. He begins by discussing performance to get the other man's attention. The body paragraphs of your essay also need to work together to convince your audience of the validity of your thesis sentence and how your research proves it.

Conclusion

After you have proved your main and sub-points in the body paragraphs, you need to end your paper by reminding the audience of the points you made. Think of the conclusion paragraph as a pyramid on its base. It starts with a restatement of the thesis sentence. Paraphrase the main point of your paper and then move on to more general points that you want to make about the subject. Does your research reveal something about a historical period, an author or a book? Explain the significance of what you have done in your paper. Highlight the main points you proved and then make a final generalization about your discipline, the subject or the primary text.

## The Resources

The following resources offer more information about how to use your research to prove your thesis and the main points in the paper:

*http://writing.colostate.edu/tools.cfm*

This Website from Colorado State University offers students from any school the opportunity to save their notes, bibliography and paper online in a database. Students can then work on their research paper from anywhere that has a computer and an Internet connection.

*http://nutsandbolts.washcoll.edu/style.html*

This Website from Michael Harvey offers fun and interesting commentary about writing a paper with research and using that research to make a point.

*www.robertniles.com/stats/*

Students who need to use statistics in their research paper should visit this Website created by Robert Niles, a journalist and self-described computer geek. The explanations are straightforward enough for anyone who wants to understand how to quote statistical sources.

*www.unc.edu/depts/wcweb/handouts/index.html*

This Website from the Writing Center at the University of North Carolina at Chapel Hill offers information about writing for every discipline.

# Proper Paper
# Format

A harried student has a few days before her final English paper is due. She is ready to put the document into final form and print it out. She knows that she should not wait until the last minute to format her paper because bad things always seem to happen when she does.

The student has often had her printer run out of ink or her computer malfunction when a big project is due. She does not want to tempt fate. After she formats her paper and prints it out, she will do a final proofread and print a corrected copy to give to her teacher.

## The Challenge

Writing a paper can be difficult and time-consuming. After all that work, the assignment is not complete until students have formatted their paper. Computers make this process much easier, but they also can add to the level of difficulty.

Students need to learn how to use their word processing software to include footnotes, page numbers and other formatting options that will make the paper look presentable. Using the technology wisely and proofreading the paper once or twice will ensure that everything is correct.

## The Facts

Students should complete their papers at lease 1 day before the due date. This extra time is necessary so that students can check the finer points of their essays and make sure that the formatting is correct. Think of formatting as the appropriate attire for prom. Students who come in blue jeans and a T-shirt tend to stick out. The same is true of a brilliant research paper that is formatted badly. You want the piece to look as well-organized and professional as the content within so you do not draw the wrong kind of attention to it.

Make sure that your papers do not have any of the following telltale signs of a rushed job:

Spelling errors

Students who write their papers in a hurry tend to wait until the last minute to check for spelling errors. The spell-checker programs for word processing software are good, but they cannot identify correctly spelled words that are used incorrectly. For example, a spell-checker will not catch if you type the word too when you mean to or two.

Grammar check programs are also helpful, but they do not usually catch misuses of to, too and two or there, they're and their. The English language is so complex that no grammar checker yet has been able to keep all the rules straight. While the sophistication of these programs is growing, they are still very limited.

Incorrect formatting

Incorrect formatting is a dead giveaway that you finished your paper in the last 5 minutes. Software glitches frequently occur when you are really counting on the programs to run smoothly.

Few references or citations

Teachers know that papers with few citations were probably written over the weekend or overnight. Do not give them the opportunity to deduct points for lack of research or adequate references.

Difficulties with past and present tense

Your teacher will quickly figure out if your paper has never been revised. If some paragraphs are in past tense–the reader tried to understand her point but failed–and some are in present tense–the reader tries to understand her point but fails–the teacher will know that you rushed to get the paper done and will deduct points accordingly.

Fewer action verbs than state of being verbs

State of being verbs include is, are, have, feel, etc. They tend to be boring when used over and over again. Action verbs are more interesting and make your paper sound better. Too many boring verbs will alert the teacher that you did not revise your paper.

## The Solutions

The correct format for your paper may be determined by your teacher or by your college. Some colleges have specific formatting rules that are used across the institution. Some teachers have a format that they prefer. Make sure to check whether a specific format is required. In general, the following basic formatting tips apply:

Paper size and color

Use plain, white paper that is 8.5 inches by 11 inches. A good quality paper will make your printer work better and produce a research paper that looks substantial. Paper that is too thin looks bad and often gets jammed in the printer.

Double-space

Double-space your paper throughout. Some disciplines, such as English, have specific formatting styles for quotations.

One-inch or larger margins

Your teacher may indicate the margins. In general, a one-inch margin is used on all four sides. Using 1.25-inch margins on the left and right makes papers slightly longer and gives the teacher a little more room to make comments.

One space after each sentence

The usual rule is to use only one space between sentences. However, check with your teacher. Some teachers still prefer two spaces between sentences because they learned to type on a typewriter instead of a keyboard.

Header or footer

Depending on your school style or your teacher's instructions, you may want to include a header, footer or both on your paper. If your teacher falls and all the term papers get mixed together, you want yours to be easy to identify. Make sure that your name, class number and your teacher's name are on every page.

Page numbers

If your teacher or school does not have specific rules about page numbers, put them in the upper, right-hand corner of your paper. This way, the teacher can see them easily as he or she reads your paper.

Type style and size

Most papers are written in 12-point type. The most common typeface is Times New Roman. Do not use any font that is italic or difficult to read. Your teacher will be reading many term papers, so make it easy on his or her eyes.

Tabs

Unless your teacher says otherwise, tabs are set at 0.5-inch intervals.

Charts and graphs

Make sure to put page numbers on any charts or graphs in your paper and make sure that they fall all on one page. They will be difficult to read if they are split between pages.

Correct formatting of quotations
> Check with your school, your teacher and your discipline to see how quotations should be formatted. Every discipline has different rules, and many English teachers have their own rules.

Footnotes or endnotes
> Make sure that you know how your teacher wants you to handle footnotes. Are you supposed to put them all at the end as endnotes? This is much easier to do. Are you supposed to use footnotes at the bottom of each page? This can be a little tricky in many word processing programs. Are you supposed to include all your citations within the text? This is easy too, but it tends to make your paper longer.

Title page
> A title page is a nice touch, so create one unless your teacher forbids it. Do not use fancy type or colors.

Fasteners
> Some professors are picky about how your paper is fastened. Stapling makes the most sense and will keep the pages from getting lost. However, some instructors prefer a single paperclip in the upper, left-hand corner.

## The Resources

The following Websites, books and other resources offer more information about the correct format for a paper:

*http://writing2.richmond.edu/writing/wweb/rushed.html*

> This Website from the Writer's Web at the University of Richmond offers a multitude of writing samples and worksheets to help students fix everything from comma splices to gerund trouble. In addition, this site features excellent information about paper formats.

*www.wisc.edu/writing/Handbook/CommonErrors_Frag.html*

> This Website from the Writing Center at the University of Wisconsin-Madison offers an editing checklist including 12 common errors in college papers. Students can find examples of every error along with good advice about how to fix each one.

*http://grammar.ccc.commnet.edu/grammar/format.htm*

> This Website from Capital Community College offers information on all aspects of writing an essay and a research paper. This particular page focuses on formatting a paper for college classes.

won the game. Now it is clear who the actors are and what they did.

When English teachers talk about weak verbs, they mean state of being verbs versus active verbs. State of being verbs such as is, was, were, have, etc. are boring because they do not indicate any action. These verbs are acceptable in combination with active verbs. Otherwise, the weak verbs can take over a paper and make each paragraph seem exactly like the one before.

4. Big words

Sometimes writers think that they can impress teachers by using big words in their essays. Some teachers mark this as wordiness, but the issue is slightly different. Using big words alone will not impress teachers. Teachers are more impressed with clear, concise sentences that make insightful points than in impressive erudition.

Students can use big words in moderation if they truly understand what those words mean. However, adding them into a paper just to impress the teacher is a bad idea. Students are better advised to work on the structure of their papers and the clarity of their examples. Teachers appreciate good writing, but they are likely to deduct points for words that the student misuses in the paper.

## The Resources

The following resources offer more information about writing style:

*http://essayinfo.com/sguides/myths.php*

This Webpage from the Essay Writing Center offers a complete list of the 11 myths of writing.

*www.dartmouth.edu/%7Ewriting/materials/student/ac_paper/style.shtml*

This Website from Dartmouth University offers an interesting way to look at sentence style. The seven principles are insightful and helpful.

*http://essayinfo.com/sguides/index.php*

This Website from the Essay Writing Center offers many writing tips. Their style guide sheets are useful.

*www.ctl.ua.edu/CTLStudyAids/StudySkillsFlyers/Reading/interpretingwritingtechniques.htm*

This Website from the University of Alabama Center for Teaching and Learning offers excellent explanations of difficult writing topics such as mood, tone and point of view.

# A Basic Style Sheet for Writers

A student in junior college received her English paper back. While she did fairly well, she is concerned about all of the red ink on the essay. Her teacher marked the paper five times for wordiness, twice for using the wrong tone and asked her to work on her style.

The student is unsure of what her teacher means. Does wordiness mean that her paper is too long or she is using big words incorrectly? What exactly does tone mean in a paper? She wants to improve her writing but does not know what her teacher is trying to tell her.

## The Challenge

Writing style can be difficult to define because it is subjective. While most professors agree about what good style is, they may disagree over the problems with a student's paper. In general, style is not the exact words that a writer uses, but the way the writer uses them. No two writers have the same style. In fact, no two writers will approach a subject the same way.

Students must find a style or voice that feels comfortable but is not unnatural. Many students think that they must sound much older than their years when writing academic papers. This leads students to show off their vocabularies instead of their critical thinking skills. The best students use a formal style that is still interesting to read.

## The Facts

Over the years, many silly rules have been created for the sole purpose of causing students to write in a stilted, formal style that no one uses anymore. Using long sentences, formal diction and difficult stylistic rules is a holdover from the Victorians. Today's writers can dispense with the following five writing myths:

Myth 1: Begin sentences with and, but or because.

This was one of the oldest and best-loved rules of the Victorian writers.

Today, most English teachers allow their students to begin a sentence with any of these words. And it is a good thing. However, before you break this rule with abandon, find out your English instructor's pet peeves about writing. If he or she still believes in this rule, you need to follow it.

Myth 2: End a sentence with a preposition.

Writers from Chaucer to Churchill have broken this rule, but many English teachers still teach it. Prepositions are small connecting words such as in, on, of, about, over, under, etc. Check with your professor to be sure. If your teacher agrees, then feel free to find out what this rule is all about.

Myth 3: Use contractions.

Contractions have not always been popular. They are shortened versions of words such as can't instead of cannot and won't instead of will not. Some teachers still believe that writers should not use contractions in formal writing. Find out what your professor thinks.

Myth 4: Use I or me.

Academic writers used to find it difficult to create sentences that did not use I or me. Many times they created long, complex sentences using such phrases as one does not or one finds oneself in the position of. These days, writers are allowed to use I and me because these pronouns allow the construction of simple, elegant sentences.

Myth 5: Write a paragraph with only one sentence.

Although most English teachers do not want you to do it more than once or twice in an essay, students usually are allowed to write one sentence paragraphs.

## The Solutions

Many components play a part in a writer's style. Four of the most important building blocks of style are listed below:

1. Tone

Tone is the way that the writer shades words in the essay. Tone also includes diction, or the way the writer refers to the audience or reader. Academic writing is considered to be formal. The problem is that no two people will define the word formal in the same way.

In general, formal style requires writers to find a happy medium between two extremes. The extreme of formal is the stilted writing of the Victorian essayists who were not allowed to refer to themselves as I or me and always wrote as if their reader was the Queen of England. The other extreme is the blog or Website writer who writes as if he or she is

chatting with friends over lunch.

When in doubt about the tone to take, be conservative. Think of the words you might use to talk to your grandparents or a much older relative. Older people generally do not understand the latest slang or trendy acronyms. Pretend that your audience is just as particular as your grandparents.

2. Wordiness

When English teachers talk to students about wordiness, they generally mean that the student is using too many words or inappropriate ones. Too many words may mean that the student is using more prepositional phrases, adjectives or adverbs than needed, and these extra words are clogging up the sentences. One good way to solve the problem of too many words is to opt for a more journalistic style and create more subject-verb-object sentences.

Wordiness also can indicate that the student is using inappropriate words in the paper, such as clichés, redundant words or too many qualifiers. Clichés are phrases that have been used so frequently that they have lost most of their meaning. For example: Jane Austen's character cuts it too close for comfort when she turns down an offer of marriage. The phrase cuts it too close for comfort is inappropriate for a college essay.

Redundant words include two words that mean the same thing or extra words that are not needed. For example: as regards Sonya, she felt that it was right and proper for us to turn in our papers late due to the fact that the dog ate our homework. The words as regards, right and proper and due to the fact that are redundant in this sentence. A better sentence would be the following: Sonya and I turned in our papers late because the dog ate our homework.

Qualifiers are words such as quite, very, really, mostly, possibly, etc. These words often add nothing to a sentence but word count. For example: Raoul was quite delighted about the really excellent opportunity we had to go to the state championships. A better sentence would be the following: Raoul was delighted about our opportunity to go to the state championships.

3. Passive voice and weak verbs

Teachers usually mark a sentence as passive voice when a writer loses track of the actor in a sentence. Most good sentences have an actor doing something. In a sentence using passive voice, the actor is obscured or lost altogether. For example: the game was won by the freshman girls. This sentence would be clearer if it read as follows: the freshman girls

# 50

# Using the Library

A liberal arts major is writing a paper for his English class. He started by doing all his research on the Internet. He found many good Websites, but his teacher requires that all papers also include books and journal articles in the bibliography.

The student does not know how to find information in the college library. He understands how the public library works, but the library at his university is large and complicated.

## The Challenge

Most college students have experience doing research in their local or high school libraries. However, they may find the large college and university libraries disconcerting.

In addition to books, periodicals and scholarly journals, college libraries also have access to a number of databases, interlibrary loan and specialized search engines. In addition, college libraries employ a number of reference librarians to help students and faculty find what they are looking for.

## The Facts

### Primary vs. Secondary Research

The first thing that students need to understand before going to the library is the difference between primary and secondary research. Primary research is the basic building block of a student's work on a paper. Primary sources help students to understand another period in history because they were written during that period or by someone who lived during that time. For example, *Pride and Prejudice* is a primary source because it was written by Jane Austen in 1813.

Secondary research includes books and articles about the primary source. For example, many scholars have written books and articles about Jane Austen's work and the world that she lived in. Other scholars have written about the position of women in Austen's time. All of these secondary resources try to analyze or interpret the primary source.

## Library Organization

Libraries can be organized in one of two methods: Dewey Decimal System or Library of Congress. Most public and high school libraries use the Dewey Decimal System. Most college and university libraries use the Library of Congress method.

Students who are used to their local or high school libraries will need to become accustomed to the new organization of their college library in order to find materials successfully.

Dewey Decimal System (DDC)
> The DDC divides the whole world of information into topic areas. The 10 topics are as follows:
> - 000 computer science information and general works
> - 100 philosophy and religion
> - 200 religion
> - 300 social sciences
> - 400 language
> - 500 science
> - 600 technology
> - 700 arts and recreation
> - 800 literature
> - 900 history and geography
>
> Each of these 10 topics can be subdivided into 10 topics, and those 10 topics can be subdivided again into 10 topics. These sub-subtopics can be divided further if necessary.

Library of Congress (LOC)
> The LOC system is organized differently. In this system, a letter represents each subject area as follows:
> - A general works
> - B philosophy, religion
> - C auxiliary sciences of history–biography, etc.
> - D history–old world
> - E-F history–new world–Americas
> - G geography, anthropology, recreation
> - H social sciences–general
> - J political science
> - K law
> - L education
> - M music
> - N arts–architecture, sculpture, drawing, painting

- P language and literature
- Q science
- R medicine
- S agriculture
- T technology–general
- U military science
- V naval science
- Z bibliography, library science

## The Solutions

The following list includes information about accessing each type of library resource:

Books

Books used to be the basic resource of libraries. Now libraries include books in their collections, but they also offer a wide range of electronic information.

The best way to find books in today's library is to use the online or electronic card catalog. An online catalog can be searched from the Internet. An electronic catalog must be used within the library itself. In addition to the information the library owns, students can get access to books owned by other college libraries. A system called interlibrary loan allows students at one college or university to borrow books from another. This is especially useful if the other library has a better collection than your library does.

Periodicals

Periodicals include magazines, newspapers and journals. They are usually published several times a year or monthly, and they offer the most up-to-date information on the topic. A book can be obsolete by the time it is published, but a current periodical usually contains information that is no more than a month old.

Periodicals can be searched in two ways. Students can use a database to find articles written on a particular subject, or they can use a reference book called *The Reader's Guide to Periodical Literature*. The database is much easier to use. However, if your library does not have enough computer terminals, you can use the print version.

Students often turn to scholarly publications when writing a research paper. These are journals that are written for faculty members and students in a particular field. For example, there are journals in literature, science and every other discipline. Students will need the journals specific to their subject.

Once you find articles that are appropriate for your paper, you need to find out if your library owns them. In most college libraries, you can search for this in the electronic card catalog.

Databases

For some subjects, students will need to use specific databases to find information. Students who need to use these resources must understand how to create and define a search to find what they want while omitting items that they do not want. Many databases use a method called Boolean operators to create searches. If you understand how these work, you can construct efficient searches.

For example, if you wanted to find journal articles about Jane Austen, and you type in her name, you would come up with thousands of hits. You probably do not have time to sift through that many articles. But if you wanted articles that discuss her novel *Pride and Prejudice* from a feminist perspective, you might use a search parameter such as the following: Jane Austen and Pride and Prejudice and feminism. The Boolean operator narrows your search because you get only those articles about Jane Austen that are also about both *Pride and Prejudice* and feminism.

If that search did not turn up enough articles, you could broaden your search. Your search might look like the following: Jane Austen and Pride and Prejudice or feminism. This will include all the articles about *Pride and Prejudice* and those about feminism in Jane Austen's works.

If you want to limit or eliminate information, you can use not. For example, if you wanted to search Jane Austen and feminism excluding articles about *Pride and Prejudice*, your search would look like the following: Jane Austen and feminism not Pride and Prejudice.

## The Resources

The following Websites, books and other resources offer more information about doing research and using it to write a paper:

*www.uah.edu/library/research_assistance/guides/library_resources.htm*

This Website from the University of Alabama in Huntsville offers a huge list of library resources and how to use them.

*www.lib.uconn.edu/using/*

This Website for the University of Connecticut libraries includes descriptions of many types of database searches and how to construct them.

# Index

# Smart, Friendly and Informative

The *50 plus one* series are thorough and detailed guides covering a wide range of topics—both personal and business related, supplying you, the reader, the information and resources you need and want in an easy-to-read format.

## 50 plus one Greatest Cities In the World You Should Visit
*by Paul J. Christopher*

Part travel book, part wish book. *50 plus one Greatest Cities in the World You Should Visit* is an intimate, easy and satisfying visit to the world's most wonderful cities. Making plans to travel? Just curious about what makes the world tick? Want to learn more about the great cultural, artistic, culinary and business centers of the world? This is the perfect book for you.

## 50 plus one Greatest Sports Heroes of All Times
**(North American edition)**
*by Paul J. Christopher*

Hold It! You really think we can come up with the greatest sports heroes of all time? Well, we can and we have! Our heroes cut across all sports and are not limited to the most popular spectator sports. On occasion our heroes go back several generations, not just the names in the papers or the sports talk shows.

## 50 plus one Questions When Buying a Car
*by Stephen Edwards*

*50 plus one Questions When Buying a Car* is the perfect self-help guide for every potential car buyer, whether you are buying new or pre-owned vehicles. How do you tell if a used car was in an accident? What features on a new car provide good values? What is the best way to finance a car? This book could save you hundreds or thousands of dollars over the many cars you will buy in your lifetime.

## 50 plus one Great Books You Should Have Read
**(and probably didn't)**
by George Walsh

*50 plus one Great Books You Should Have Read (and probably didn't)* is a masterpiece of information for individuals who want to expand their horizons or simply impress friends. Walsh and his advisory panel selected literary works, which have had the greatest impact on writing, government, international politics, religion, and the arts and sciences. International in scope, the books chosen for this list have survived centuries and are considered essential for a liberal education.

## Titles from Encouragement Press

Available from bookstores everywhere or directly from Encouragement Press. Bulk discounts are available, for information please call 1.253.303.0033

### 50 plus one Series

| Title | Price | Qty. | Subtotal |
|---|---|---|---|
| Greatest Cities in the World Y | | | |
| Tips When Remodeling Your | | | |
| Greatest Sports Heroes of All | | | |
| Tips to Building A Retiremen | | | |
| Ways To Improve Your Study | | | |
| Tips When Hiring & Firing Em | | | |
| Questions When Buying a Ca | | | |
| Tips to Preventing Identity Theft | $14.95 U.S./$19.95 Can. | | |
| Great Books You Should Have Read (and probably didn't) | $14.95 U.S./$19.95 Can. | | |
| Questions to Ask Your Doctor | $14.95 U.S./$19.95 Can. | | |
| | Subtotal | | |
| | IL residents add 8.75% sales tax | | |
| | Shipping & Handling* | | |
| | Total | | |

**\* Shipping & Handling**

| U.S. Orders: | Canadian Orders: |
|---|---|
| $3.35 for first book | $7.00 for first book |
| $2.00 for ea. add'l add book | $5.00 for ea. add'l book |

## 4 Ways to Order

**Phone:** 1.773.262.6565

**Web:** *www.encouragementpress.com*

**Fax:** 1.773.262.9765

**Mail:** Encouragement Press LLC
1261 West Glenlake
Chicago, IL 60660

Please make checks payable to:
Encouragement Press, LLC
*(Orders must be prepaid. We regret that
we are unable to ship orders without
payment or purchase order)*

**Payment Method (check one)**
❏ Check enclosed  ❏ Visa  ❏ MasterCard

_____

**card number**

_____

**signature**

_____

**Name as it appears on card**

**expiration date** _____

**P.O. #**_____

Encouragement Press, LLC
1261 West Glenlake • Chicago, IL 60660 • *sales@encouragementpress.com*